The VEGAN INSTANT POT *Cookbook*

~ 500 ~

Wholesome, Indulgent Plant-Based Recipes for the Healthy Cook's Kitchen

Dr. Elizabeth Perry Md

TABLE OF CONTENTS

DESCRIPTION

Vegan lifestyle consists of whole food and plants, and thus, it has compelling benefits like weight loss, reducing risk of heart diseases, cancer, Alzheimer's disease, and many more.

If you considering going vegan, then you are not alone. The start of a vegan diet is not easy and can be overwhelming as you won't able to devour your favorite cheese sandwich or chicken recipes. Indeed, a vegan diet is difficult for those individuals who grew up eating animal food and products regularly.

So, is it worth it? Yes, the transition to an entirely plant-based diet is so much more despite amazing health benefits. Vegans have reported their sense of taste heightened, and the nutritious vegan foods bring so much pleasure. And, just in a few weeks, vegans tend to forget animal foods and junk foods. Individuals also feel an immediate increase in their energy level when they go vegan.

Moreover, the fiber intake from the diet eliminate gas problems and improve bloating. The most significant physical change you will see along with weight loss will be your skin. Vegan diet clears the complexion, and your skin will never look better than before.

This guide brings you the best collection of vegan recipes which include;

- Breakfast
- Mains
- Sides
- Vegetables
- Beans, grains & pasta
- Soups and Stews
- Snacks
- Desserts

Start the vegetarianism diet gradually. This will help you more consciously choose food and reduce the level of stress for your body. Step by step you will figure out the principles of right vegan diet and this cookbook will be a good guide to the world of delicious vegan food recipes!

INTRODUCTION

Presently, the world is divided into people who support veganism and those who are against the complete abandonment of animal products. It is possible to say that this vegan recipe guide can be a good gift to everyone who loves delicious food. These days veganism is a sought-after way of life. More often people refuse to consume all types of meat and dairy products and limit yourself with fruits, vegetables, and another produces. It is true that thanks to the vegan lifestyle, you can improve your health and feel much better. Scientifically proved that total refusing from any type of meat and dairy products can help fight with Type 2 diabetes, reduce Low-Density Lipoprotein (LDL) level, and helps to decrease blood pressure. Veganism is a good way to raise the level of antioxidant, vitamins, minerals, and dietary fiber in the body. This happens due to increased fruit, vegetable, grains, legumes, and beans consumption.

However, veganism can be harmful to you, cause some inconvenience, and make significant changes in your body. Every diet needs a special meal plan that is developed individually for the right saturation of the body with all nutrients. If you have any health problems, a vegan diet can interfere with your health. It is highly recommended to make full medical body examinations and consult the doctor about the possible consequences of changing the diet. The inconveniences can happen while eating out. Single restaurants and cafes can boast a wide range of high-quality vegan meals. There is a solution that is used by a lot of vegans: to take food with yourself. Doing it you won't miss the mealtime and stay full.

SUPERFOOD COOKIES

Preparation Time: 15 minutes

Cooking Time: 6 minutes

Servings: 4

Ingredients:

- ½ cup oats
- 1 tablespoon pumpkin seeds, chopped
- 1 tablespoon sunflower seeds
- 1 tablespoon almonds, chopped
- 1 tablespoon cranberries
- ½ teaspoon ground nutmeg
- 3 tablespoon aquafaba
- 1 tablespoon almond flour
- ¼ cup golden syrup
- Cooking spray

Directions:

1. In the mixing bowl mix up together all the ingredients except cooking spray.
2. Then with the help of 2 spoons make medium size balls and place them on the instant pot baking trivet.
3. Spray the cookies with cooking spray and place in the instant pot.
4. Set manual mode (High pressure) and close the lid.
5. Cook the cookies for 6 minutes. Then make low pressure release for 10 minutes.
6. Chill the cookies till the room temperature.

Nutrition Values: Calories 124, fat 2.9, fiber 1.5, carbs 24, protein 2.4

BROWN RICE CONGEE

Preparation Time: 20 minutes

Cooking Time: 25 minutes

Servings: 4

Ingredients:

- ½ cup of brown rice
- ½ cup basmati rice
- 4 cups mushroom broth
- 1 teaspoon Pink salt
- 4 tablespoon quinoa
- 1 teaspoon turmeric
- ½ teaspoon smoked paprika

Directions:

1. Put all the ingredients in the instant pot bowl and stir gently.
2. Close the lid and set High pressure on Manual mode.
3. Cook the meal for 25 minutes and then make the quick pressure release for 15 minutes.
4. Stir rice congee carefully and transfer into the serving plates.

Nutrition Values: Calories 222, fat 1.5, fiber 2.1, carbs 45.9, protein 5

POTATO CHAAT

Preparation Time: 10 minutes

Cooking Time: 43 minutes

Servings: 5

Ingredients:

- 3 russet potatoes, peeled, chopped
- 1 tablespoon olive oil
- ½ tablespoon garam masala
- ½ teaspoon ground cumin
- ½ teaspoon dried basil
- ½ teaspoon dried oregano
- ½ teaspoon garlic powder
- 1 zucchini, chopped
- 1 carrot, peeled, chopped
- 1 sweet red pepper, chopped
- ¼ teaspoon ground cinnamon
- ½ cup of water
- 1 cup collards, chopped

Directions:

1. Put potatoes in the instant pot bowl and add olive oil and garam masala.
2. Mix up potatoes with the help of a spatula and cook on Saute mode for 5 minutes.
3. Meanwhile, in the mixing bowl combine together ground cumin, basil, oregano, garlic powder, and ground cinnamon.
4. Add the spices in the instant pot bowl and mix up.
5. Then add chopped carrot and zucchini. Cook it for 2 minutes more.
6. Pour water in the instant pot bowl and add collards.
7. Close the lid and cook the meal on Saute mode for 35 minutes.

Nutrition Values: Calories 136, fat 3.2, fiber 4.6, carbs 25.3, protein 3.3

ALMOND MILK COCKTAIL

Preparation Time: 10 minutes

Cooking Time: 3 minutes

Servings: 4

Ingredients:

- 2 cups almonds
- 4 cups of water
- 2 tablespoons honey
- ½ teaspoon ground cinnamon
- 4 teaspoon walnuts, chopped

Directions:

1. Place the almonds in the instant pot bowl and add 1 cup of water.
2. Close the lid and cook almonds on Manual mode (High pressure) for 3 minutes.
3. Then make quick pressure release. Strain the almonds and transfer them in the blender.
4. Add all remaining water and blend the mixture until smooth and white color.
5. Then strain the liquid to get almond milk.
6. Mix up together almond milk, chopped walnuts, and honey.
7. Pour the cocktail in the glasses and sprinkle with cinnamon.

Nutrition Values: Calories 324, fat 25.3, fiber 6.3, carbs 19.3, protein 10.7

BANANA ROLLS

Preparation Time: 25 minutes

Cooking Time: 25 minutes

Servings: 4

Ingredients:

- ½ teaspoon yeast
- 1/3 cup warm water
- 1 cup wheat flour
- ½ teaspoon salt
- 3 tablespoon white sugar
- 2 bananas, mashed
- 1 teaspoon vanilla extract
- 1 tablespoon brown sugar
- 1 tablespoon olive oil

Directions:

1. Mix up together warm water, yeast, and ½ cup of wheat flour.
2. Add white sugar and stir the mixture until smooth.
3. Leave it for 10 minutes.
4. Then add salt, vanilla extract, and all remaining flour.
5. Knead soft and non-sticky dough.
6. Leave the dough for 10 minutes to rest in the warm place.
7. Meanwhile, mix up together brown sugar and mashed bananas.
8. Roll up the dough and spread it with mashed banana mixture.
9. Roll it and cut into the buns.
10. Brush the instant pot bowl with a ½ tablespoon of olive oil.
11. Place the rolls in the instant pot and brush with remaining olive oil.
12. Close the lid and set manual mode (High pressure).
13. Cook rolls for 25 minutes. Then make quick pressure release. The time of cooking depends on rolls size.

Nutrition Values: Calories 243, fat 4, fiber 2.5, carbs 48.9, protein 4.1

BREAKFAST BOWL

Preparation Time: 10 minutes

Cooking Time: 14 minutes

Servings: 3

Ingredients:

- ½ cup quinoa, soaked
- 1 ½ cup almond milk
- 1 tablespoon coconut shred
- 2 teaspoon honey
- 1 teaspoon vanilla extract
- ½ teaspoon ground cinnamon
- 1 tablespoon hemp seeds

1. **Directions:**
2. Place quinoa and almond milk in the instant pot bowl.
3. Add vanilla extract and stir gently.
4. Close the lid and set Rice mode. Cook quinoa for 14 minutes (Low pressure).
5. Transfer cooked quinoa in the big bowl and add honey, coconut shred, and ground cinnamon.
6. Add hemp seeds and mix up the mixture well.
7. Transfer hot quinoa into the serving

bowls.

Nutrition Values: Calories 459, fat 35.4, fiber 5.7, carbs 30.8, protein 8.8

TOFU OMELET

Preparation Time: 10 minutes

Cooking Time: 8 minutes

Servings: 3

Ingredients:

- 8 oz firm tofu
- ¾ cup aquafaba
- 1 tablespoon chickpea flour
- 1 tablespoon cornflour
- ¼ cup almond milk
- 1 tablespoon wheat flour
- ½ teaspoon salt
- ¾ teaspoon turmeric
- ½ teaspoon dried basil
- 1 teaspoon olive oil
- 1 tablespoon fresh parsley, chopped

Directions:

1. In the blender mix up together firm tofu, aquafaba, chickpea flour, cornflour, almond milk, wheat flour, salt, and turmeric.
2. Blend the mixture until you get a smooth yellow liquid that looks like an omelet.
3. Brush the instant pot bowl with the olive oil from inside and pour tofu mixture.
4. Add parsley and dried basil and stir gently.

5. Close the lid and cook the omelet on Manual mode (High pressure) and cook it for 8 minutes. Then make quick pressure release.

Nutrition Values: Calories 148, fat 9.9, fiber 2.3, carbs 9.2, protein 8

TAPIOCA PORRIDGE

Preparation Time: 5 minutes

Cooking Time: 17 minutes

Servings: 4

Ingredients:

- ½ cup tapioca pearls
- 1 tablespoon tapioca flour
- 2 cups almond milk
- 1 tablespoon honey

Directions:

1. In the instant pot, mix up together tapioca pearls, tapioca flour, and almond milk.
2. Close the lid and cook on High for 17 minutes. Then allow natural pressure release for 10 minutes.
3. Open the lid and add honey. Stir the porridge until homogenous.
4. Transfer the cooked porridge in the serving bowls

Nutrition Values: Calories 366, fat 28.6, fiber 2.8, carbs 29.5, protein 2.8

ZUCCHINI FRITTATA

Preparation Time: 7 minutes

Cooking Time: 12 minutes

Servings: 5

Ingredients:

- 6 oz firm tofu
- 1 zucchini
- 1 red onion, diced
- ¼ cup almond milk
- 1 teaspoon salt
- 1 teaspoon ground black pepper
- 2 tablespoons wheat flour
- ½ teaspoon olive oil

Directions:

1. Grate zucchini and scramble tofu.
2. Mix up together zucchini, tofu, onion, and almond milk.
3. Add salt, ground black pepper, and wheat flour. Mix up the mixture until homogenous.
4. Brush the instant pot bowl with olive oil from inside.
5. Then transfer zucchini mixture in it. Flatten it with the help of a spatula.
6. Close the lid and set Manual mode (High pressure).
7. Cook frittata for 12 minutes. Then allow natural pressure release for 10 minutes.
8. The frittata should be served warm.

Nutrition Values: Calories 83, fat 4.9, fiber 1.7, carbs 7.3, protein 4.1

APPLE CREAM OF WHEAT

Preparation Time: 8 minutes

Cooking Time: 7 hours

Servings: 3

Ingredients:

- ½ cup cream of wheat
- 2 ½ cup almond milk
- 4 teaspoon sugar
- ½ teaspoon ground cinnamon
- 1 granny smith apple

Directions:

1. Put cream of wheat and almond milk in the instant pot bowl.
2. Add sugar and cinnamon. Mix up gently. Close the lid.
3. Set the Rice mode (Low pressure) and cook the meal for 7 hours.
4. When the cream of wheat is cooked: slice the apple.
5. Place the cream of wheat in the bowls and garnish with apple.

Nutrition Values: Calories 469, fat 36.2, fiber 5.4, carbs 36.7, protein 5.8

OATMEAL MUFFINS

Preparation Time: 10 minutes

Cooking Time: 8 minutes

Servings: 6

Ingredients:

- 1 cup quick oats
- 2 tablespoon white sugar
- 1 teaspoon vanilla extract
- ¼ cup wheat flour
- 1 teaspoon almond butter
- 2 tablespoon coconut milk
- 1 oz walnuts, chopped
- Cooking spray

Directions:

1. In the mixing bowl combine together dry ingredients: white sugar, quick oats, wheat flour, and chopped walnuts.
2. Mix up the mixture well and add almond butter, vanilla extract, and coconut milk.
3. Stir the mixture with the help of a spoon.
4. Spray muffin molds with the cooking spray.
5. Scoop the oat mixture in the molds and press gently.
6. Cover the molds with foil and pin it with the help of a toothpick.
7. Transfer it in the instant pot bowl and close the lid.
8. Cook muffins on High (Manual mode) for 8 minutes. Use quick pressure release.

Nutrition Values: Calories 145, fat 6.4, fiber 2.2, carbs 18.6, protein 4.2

TEMPEH BOWL

Preparation Time: 10 minutes

Cooking Time: 11 minutes

Servings: 5

Ingredients:

- ½ cup potatoes, chopped
- 1 cup spinach, chopped
- ½ cup of water
- 1 teaspoon Italian seasoning
- 1 teaspoon sriracha
- 1 tablespoon soy sauce
- 1 teaspoon minced garlic
- 1 teaspoon salt
- 8 oz tempeh, chopped
- ½ cup kale, chopped
- 1 teaspoon nutritional yeast

Directions:

1. In the mixing bowl mix up together salt, Italian seasoning, and chopped potato.
2. Insert the steamer rack in the instant pot bowl.
3. Place the potatoes and water in the bottom of the instant pot bowl.
4. Then take round instant pot pan and place tempeh inside.
5. Add sriracha, soy sauce, and minced garlic. Mix it up.
6. Then add kale and spinach.
7. Sprinkle the greens with nutritional yeast and cover with foil. Make the pins in the foil with the help of a knife or toothpick.
8. Place the pan on the steamer rack and close the instant pot lid.
9. Cook the meal for 11 minutes on Manual mode (High pressure).
10. Then make quick pressure release.
11. Place the meal in the bowls by layers: the layer of potatoes, then greens, and then tempeh.

Nutrition Values: Calories 111, fat 5.3, fiber 0.8, carbs 8.6, protein 9.6

TENDER TOFU CUBES

Preparation Time: 10 minutes

Cooking Time: 15 minutes

Servings: 4

Ingredients:

- 15 oz firm tofu, cubed
- 1 teaspoon curry powder
- ½ teaspoon salt
- 1 teaspoon garlic powder
- ½ onion, diced
- 1 teaspoon smoked paprika
- 1 teaspoon almond butter
- 1 cup of coconut yogurt

Directions:

1. Preheat instant pot bowl on Saute mode.
2. When it shows "hot" toss almond butter inside.
3. Melt it and add diced onion, garlic powder, salt, curry powder, and smoked paprika.
4. Stir the ingredients and saute for 2 minutes on Saute mode.
5. Then add firm tofu cubes and mix up well.
6. Close the lid and set Manual mode (High pressure). Cook tofu for 2 minutes and them use natural pressure release for 10 minutes.
7. Open the lid and add coconut yogurt. Mix up the meal very well.
8. Place meal in the bowls and serve when it reaches room temperature.

Nutrition Values: Calories 185, fat 10.3, fiber 2.3, carbs 12.2, protein 13.5

POTATO PANCAKES

Preparation Time: 8 minutes

Cooking Time: 15 minutes

Servings: 4

Ingredients:

- 3 potatoes, peeled
- 2 tablespoon wheat flour
- 1 teaspoon cornstarch
- 1 teaspoon salt
- ½ teaspoon ground black pepper
- 1 tablespoon chives
- 1 teaspoon fresh dill, chopped
- 1 tablespoon olive oil

Directions:

1. Grate potatoes and mix them up with wheat flour, cornstarch, salt. Ground black pepper, chives, and fresh dill.
2. Separate the mixture into 4 parts.
3. Preheat instant pot bowl till it shows "hot", and pour olive oil inside.
4. Place the first part of grated potato mixture in the instant pot bowl and flatten it to make the shape of a pancake.
5. Cook it on Saute mode for 4 minutes from each side or until "pancake" is light brown.
6. Repeat the same steps with all remaining grated potato mixture.

Nutrition Values: Calories 159, fat 3.7, fiber 4.1, carbs 29, protein 3.2

AVOCADO SANDWICHES

Preparation Time: 10 minutes

Cooking Time: 6 minutes

Servings: 2

Ingredients:

- 4 vegan bread slices
- 1 avocado, peeled
- 1 teaspoon minced garlic
- 1 tomato, chopped
- 1 tablespoon coconut oil
- 1 tablespoon chives, chopped
- 1 teaspoon smoked paprika

Directions:

1. Mash the avocado with the help of fork and transfer in the blender.
2. Add minced garlic, chopped tomato, chives, and smoked paprika.
3. Blend the mixture until smooth.
4. Then spread each bread slice with avocado mixture and make sandwiches.
5. Preheat the instant pot until it shows "Hot".
6. Place the coconut oil inside instant pot bowl and add avocado sandwiches.
7. Set Saute mode and cook them for 3 minutes from each side. Cooked sandwiches should have a light crunchy texture.

Nutrition Values: Calories 326, fat 27.3, fiber 8.1, carbs 20.6, protein 4.2

AMISH OATS.

Preparation Time: 15 Minutes

Servings: 6

Ingredients:

- 3 cups unsweetened almond milk or other non-dairy milk

- 2½ cups old-fashioned rolled oats
- 2/3 cup sweetened dried cranberries
- ½ cup packed light brown sugar or maple syrup
- ½ cup toasted slivered blanched almonds or chopped walnuts
- 2 tablespoons vegan butter, melted
- 2 teaspoons pure vanilla extract
- 1½ teaspoons ground cinnamon
- 1½ teaspoons baking powder
- ½ teaspoon salt

Directions:

1. Lightly oil your Instant Pot insert with cooking spray.
2. In a bowl mix the almond milk, butter, vanilla, sugar, baking powder, salt, and cinnamon.
3. Stir in the oats, cranberries, and nuts.
4. Seal and cook on Beans for 12 minutes.

SWEET PUMPKIN QUINOA.

Preparation Time: 45 Minutes

Servings: 4

Ingredients:

- 4 cups unsweetened almond milk
- 1 cup quinoa, rinsed and drained
- ½ cup canned solid-pack pumpkin
- ¼ cup pure maple syrup
- 1 teaspoon pure vanilla extract
- 1 teaspoon ground cinnamon
- ½ teaspoon salt

- ¼ teaspoon ground ginger
- ¼ teaspoon ground allspice
- ¼ teaspoon ground nutmeg

Directions:

1. Spray the insert of your Instant Pot with cooking oil.
2. Add the ingredients.
3. Seal and cook on Stew for 38 minutes.
4. Depressurize naturally and serve.

BREAKFAST POLENTA.

Preparation Time: 50 Minutes

Servings: 4

Ingredients:

- 4 cups water
- 1 cup medium- or coarse-ground polenta
- 1 tablespoon vegan butter
- 2 tablespoons pure maple syrup
- 1 teaspoon salt

Directions:

1. Combine the polenta, water and salt in your Instant Pot.
2. Seal and cook on Stew for 40 minutes.
3. Release the pressure naturally and stir in vegan butter and maple syrup.

MOLASSES POLENTA.

Preparation Time: 50 Minutes

Servings: 6

Ingredients:

- 3½ cups unsweetened almond milk
- 2/3 cup chopped dates
- ½ cup medium-ground cornmeal
- ¼ cup packed light brown sugar
- ¼ cup molasses
- 2 tablespoons vegan butter
- 1 teaspoon pure vanilla extract
- ½ teaspoon salt
- ½ teaspoon baking powder
- ½ teaspoon ground cinnamon
- ½ teaspoon ground ginger
- ¼ teaspoon ground nutmeg

Directions:

1. Spray your Instant Pot insert with cooking spray.
2. Warm 2 cups of the almond milk, the cornmeal, and some salt.
3. When boiling add the sugar, molasses, cinnamon, nutmeg, ginger, and dates.
4. Add another cup of almond milk, vanilla, and baking powder and mix well.
5. Add the remaining almond milk and seal.
6. Cook on Stew for 40 minutes.

CONGEE.

Preparation Time: 35 Minutes

Servings: 6

Ingredients:

- 6 cups hot vegetable broth
- 1 cup uncooked Arborio rice

- 1 small yellow onion, minced
- 1 tablespoon soy sauce
- 2 teaspoons grated fresh ginger
- 1 teaspoon salt

Directions:

1. Mix the ingredients in your Instant Pot.
2. Seal and cook on Rice.
3. Release the pressure naturally.

RENCH TOAST PUDDING.

Preparation Time: 15 Minutes

Servings: 4

Ingredients:

- 8 cups stale white Italian bread cubes
- 6 ounces soft or silken tofu, drained
- 2 cups non-dairy milk
- ½ cup packed light brown sugar
- ¼ cup pure maple syrup, plus more for serving
- ¼ cup coarsely chopped pecans or walnuts
- 1 tablespoon vegan butter
- 2 teaspoons pure vanilla extract
- 1 teaspoon ground cinnamon
- ¼ teaspoon ground nutmeg
- ¼ teaspoon salt
- ⅛ teaspoon ground allspice

Directions:

1. Oil a pan that will fit in your Instant Pot steamer basket.
2. Add the bread to the pan.

3. Blend together the tofu, vanilla, cinnamon, allspice, nutmeg, sugar, and salt. Stir in the milk and maple syrup.
4. Pour the tofu over the bread.
5. Add the minimum water to the Instant Pot and put the tray in the steamer basket.
6. Cook on Steam for 10 minutes.

BANANAS FOSTER FRENCH TOAST.

Preparation Time: 15 Minutes

Servings: 4

Ingredients:

- 8 cups stale cubed white bread
- 6 ounces firm silken tofu
- 3 ripe bananas
- 1 cup nondairy milk
- 1 cup pecan pieces
- ½ cup packed light brown sugar
- ½ cup pure maple syrup
- ⅓ cup dried banana chips
- 3 tablespoons dark rum or brandy
- 2 tablespoons vegan butter
- 2 tablespoons cornstarch
- 1 teaspoon pure vanilla extract
- ½ teaspoon salt

Directions:

1. Oil a pan that will fit in your Instant Pot steamer basket.
2. Add the bread to the pan.
3. Blend together the maple syrup,

butter, sugar, rum, bananas, tofu, milk, cornstarch, vanilla, and salt.

4. Sprinkle bananas and pecans over the bread.

5. Pour the tofu over the bread.

6. Add the minimum water to the Instant Pot and put the tray in the steamer basket.

7. Cook on Steam for 10 minutes.

VEGAN SAUSAGE SCRAMBLE.

Preparation Time: 15 Minutes

Servings: 6

Ingredients:

- 1 pound firm tofu, drained, crumbled, and squeezed dry

- 6 cups cubed French or Italian bread

- 2 cups sliced white mushrooms

- 2 cups crumbled cooked vegan sausage

- 1½ cups plain unsweetened nondairy milk

- 1 medium-size yellow onion, minced

- 1 red or green bell pepper, seeded and chopped

- 3 garlic cloves, minced

- 2 teaspoons olive oil

- ½ teaspoon ground fennel seed

- ½ teaspoon dried basil

- ¼ teaspoon red pepper flakes, or more to taste

- 3 tablespoons nutritional yeast

- 1 tablespoon cornstarch

- 1 teaspoon yellow mustard

- 1 teaspoon smoked paprika

- Salt and freshly ground black pepper

Directions:

1. Warm the oil in your Instant Pot and soften the onion for 5 minutes in it.

2. Add the garlic, mushrooms, and pepper and cook another 2 minutes.

3. Add the basil, fennel, and red pepper.

4. Pulse the tofu, milk, cornstarch, nutritional yeast, mustard, and paprika.

5. Put the bread in your Instant Pot and mix with the vegetables.

6. Pour the tofu over the bread.

7. Seal and cook on Stew for 12 minutes.

CHORIZO FRITTATA.

Preparation Time: 20 Minutes

Servings: 4

Ingredients:

- 1 pound firm tofu, well drained and lightly pressed

- 8 ounces white mushrooms, chopped

- 5 scallions, minced

- 1 cup crumbled vegan chorizo

- 1 cup shredded vegan cheese of your choice

- ½ cup vegetable broth

- ¼ cup nutritional yeast

- 2 teaspoons olive oil

- 1 tablespoon cornstarch or tapioca starch

- ½ teaspoon onion powder

- ½ teaspoon dried basil
- ½ teaspoon garlic powder
- ½ teaspoon smoked paprika
- Salt and freshly ground black pepper

Directions:

1. Blend the tofu, nutritional yeast, cornstarch, garlic powder, onion powder, basil, paprika, broth, salt and pepper.
2. Warm the oil in the base of your Instant Pot.
3. Add the scallions, chorizo, mushrooms, and some salt and pepper and cook 5 minutes.
4. Stir the chorizo and tofu mixes together.
5. Top with cheese.
6. Seal and cook on Stew for 15 minutes.
7. Remove and cut into slices.

ARTICHOKE FRITTATA.

Preparation Time: 22 Minutes

Servings: 4

Ingredients:

- 1 pound firm tofu, well drained and lightly pressed
- 2 cups canned or thawed frozen artichoke hearts, chopped
- 8 ounces white mushrooms, thinly sliced or chopped
- 5 scallions, minced
- 1 cup vegetable broth
- ½ cup shredded vegan cheese of your choice

- ⅓ cup chopped sun-dried tomatoes
- 3 tablespoons nutritional yeast
- 1 tablespoon cornstarch or tapioca starch
- 2 teaspoons olive oil
- 1 teaspoon capers, rinsed and drained
- ½ teaspoon dried thyme
- ½ teaspoon dried basil
- ½ teaspoon onion powder
- Salt and freshly ground black pepper

Directions:

1. Blend the tofu, nutritional yeast, cornstarch, onion powder, salt and pepper with 1 tablespoon tomatoes.
2. Warm the oil in the base of your Instant Pot.
3. Add the scallions, mushrooms, thyme, basil, and some salt and pepper and cook 5 minutes.
4. Stir the veg and tofu mixes together.
5. Top with cheese.
6. Seal and cook on Stew for 18 minutes.
7. Remove and cut into slices.

GREEK FRITTATA.

Preparation Time: 20 Minutes

Servings: 4

Ingredients:

- 1 pound firm tofu, well drained and lightly pressed
- 3 cups lightly packed fresh baby spinach
- ½ cup pitted kalamata olives, coarsely

chopped

- 1 small yellow onion, chopped
- 3 large garlic cloves, crushed
- 1 jarred roasted red bell pepper, chopped
- 3 tablespoons nutritional yeast
- 1 tablespoon freshly squeezed lemon juice
- 2 teaspoons olive oil
- 1 teaspoon dried basil
- 1 teaspoon dried oregano
- Salt and freshly ground black pepper

Directions:

1. Warm the oil in the base of your Instant Pot.
2. Add the onion and cook 5 minutes.
3. Add the basil, oregano, and garlic and cook another minute.
4. Blend the tofu, nutritional yeast, onion mix, lemon juice, and salt and pepper.
5. Stir the veg and tofu mixes together in the Instant Pot.
6. Seal and cook on Stew for 15 minutes.
7. Remove and cut into slices.

STEWED FALL FRUITS.

Preparation Time: 25 Minutes

Servings: 8

Ingredients:

- 3 large apples, peeled, cored, and cut into 1-inch dice
- 2 just-ripe pears, peeled, cored, and

cut into 1-inch dice

- 1 cup dried apricots, quartered
- ½ cup pitted prunes, halved
- ½ cup sweetened dried cranberries
- ¼ cup water
- ¼ cup granulated natural sugar
- 1 cinnamon stick
- Grated zest and juice of 1 lemon or orange

Directions:

1. Combine all the ingredients in your Instant Pot and mix well.
2. Seal and cook on Stew for 22 minutes.
3. Release the pressure naturally.
4. If it is not thick enough, simmer with the lid off a while.

CHAI BREAKFAST LOAF.

Preparation Time: 15 Minutes

Servings: 10

Ingredients:

- 1¾ cups unbleached all-purpose flour
- ¾ cup organic sugar
- ¾ cup non-dairy milk mixed with ½ teaspoon apple cider vinegar
- ½ cup double-strength brewed black tea
- ¼ cup vegan butter, melted and cooled
- 2 tablespoons unsweetened applesauce
- 2 tablespoons sunflower seeds

- 2 teaspoons baking powder
- 2 teaspoons pure vanilla extract
- ½ teaspoon salt
- ½ teaspoon baking soda
- ¾ teaspoon ground cinnamon
- ½ teaspoon ground cardamom
- ¼ teaspoon ground nutmeg
- ⅛ teaspoon ground cloves

Directions:

1. Lightly oil a baking tray that will fit in the steamer basket of your Instant Pot.
2. In a bowl, combine the flour, baking powder, baking soda, salt and spices.
3. In another bowl cream the sugar and butter.
4. Stir the applesauce, milk, tea, and vanilla into the butter.
5. Stir the wet mixture into the dry mixture slowly until they form a smooth mix.
6. Fold in the seeds.
7. Pour the batter into your baking tray and put the tray in your steamer basket.
8. Pour the minimum amount of water into the base of your Instant Pot and lower the steamer basket.
9. Seal and cook on Steam for 10 minutes.
10. Release the pressure quickly and set to one side to cool a little.

GRANOLA APPLES.

Preparation Time: 25 Minutes

Servings: 6

Ingredients:

- 6 Granny Smiths, washed
- 1½ cups granola
- ½ cup apple juice
- Juice of 1 lemon
- 2 tablespoons light brown sugar or granulated natural sugar
- 1½ tablespoons vegan butter, cut into 6
- ½ teaspoon ground cinnamon

Directions:

1. Core the apples most of the way down, leaving a little base so the stuffing stays put.
2. Stand your apples upright in your Instant Pot. Do not pile them on top of each other! You may need to do two batches.
3. In a bowl combine the sugar, granola, and cinnamon.
4. Stuff each apple with the mix and top with butter.
5. Pour the apple juice around the apples.
6. Seal and cook on Stew for 20 minutes.
7. Depressurize naturally.

BLACK QUINOA BREAKFAST MIX

Preparation time: 10 minutes

Cooking Time: 3 minutes

Servings: 4

Ingredients:

- 1 cup black quinoa
- 1 and ½ cups water

- A pinch of salt
- Zest from 1 lime, grated
- Juice from 1 lime
- 1 bunch parsley, chopped
- 1 tomato, chopped
- ½ cup green olives, pitted and sliced
- 1 yellow bell pepper, chopped
- 1 cucumber, chopped

Directions:

1. In your instant pot, mix quinoa with water, salt and lime zest, stir, cover and cook on High for 3 minutes.
2. Drain quinoa, transfer to a salad bowl, lime juice, parsley, tomato, olives, bell pepper and cucumber, toss well and serve for breakfast.
3. Enjoy!

Nutrition: calories 162, fat 1, fiber 3, carbs 9, protein 8

BREAKFAST BEAN SALAD

Preparation time: 10 minutes

Cooking Time: 15 minutes

Servings: 4

Ingredients:

- 1 cup chickpeas, soaked and drained
- 1 cup cranberry beans, soaked and drained
- 1 bay leaf
- 1 garlic clove, minced
- 1 and ½ cups green beans
- 2 celery stalks, chopped
- ½ red onion, chopped

- 5 tablespoons apple cider vinegar
- 4 tablespoons olive oil
- 1 tablespoon stevia
- A pinch of salt and black pepper

Directions:

1. In your instant pot, mix water with chickpeas, bay leaf and garlic and stir.
2. Add steamer basket, add cranberry and green beans inside, cover pot and cook on High for 15 minutes.
3. Drain all beans and transfer them to a salad bowl.
4. Add celery, onion, vinegar, stevia, oil, salt and pepper, toss well and serve for breakfast.
5. Enjoy!

Nutrition: calories 200, fat 4, fiber 7, carbs 20, protein 6

BREAKFAST POTATO SALAD

Preparation time: 10 minutes

Cooking Time: 5 minutes

Servings: 6

Ingredients:

- 3 pounds red potatoes, peeled and roughly chopped
- 1 small red onion, chopped
- 1 parsley bunch, chopped
- 4 tablespoons olive oil
- 4 tablespoons white wine vinegar
- A pinch of salt and black pepper
- 1 and ½ cups water

Directions:

1. Put the water in your instant pot, add steamer basket, add potatoes inside, cover and cook on High for 5 minutes.

2. Drain potatoes, transfer to a salad bowl, add salt, pepper, oil, vinegar, onion and parsley, toss well and serve for breakfast.

3. Enjoy!

Nutrition: calories 231, fat 6, fiber 4, carbs 8, protein 5

VEGGIE SALAD

Preparation time: 10 minutes

Cooking Time: 10 minutes

Servings: 4

Ingredients:

- 2 yellow bell peppers, cut into thin strips
- 2 red bell peppers, cut into thin strips
- 1 red onion, chopped
- 2 tomatoes, chopped
- 1 green bell pepper, cut into thin strips
- 1 bunch parsley, chopped
- 2 garlic cloves, minced
- A drizzle of olive oil
- A pinch of salt and pepper

Directions:

1. Set your instant pot on sauté mode, add a drizzle of oil, heat it up, add onions, stir and cook for 1 minute.

2. Add red, yellow, green peppers and garlic, stir and cook for 4 minutes more.

3. Add tomatoes, salt, pepper and parsley, stir, cover and cook on High for 5 minutes.

4. Divide into bowls and serve for breakfast.

5. Enjoy!

Nutrition: calories 100, fat 2, fiber 3, carbs 4, protein 2

ITALIAN VEGGIE MIX

Preparation time: 10 minutes

Cooking Time: 13 minutes

Servings: 4

Ingredients:

- ¼ cup olive oil
- 2 zucchinis, cut into small rounds
- 1 red bell pepper, cut into thin strips
- 1 yellow onion, cut into medium wedges
- 1 eggplant, cubed
- A pinch of salt and black pepper
- 2 potatoes, cubed
- 1 tablespoons capers
- 10 cherry tomatoes, halved
- 2 tablespoons pine nuts
- ¼ cup black olives, pitted
- 1 tablespoons raisins
- 1 basil bunch, chopped

Directions:

Set your instant pot on sauté mode, add oil, heat it up, add onion and eggplant, stir and cook for 3 minutes.

Add zucchinis and red bell pepper, stir and

cook for 3 minutes more.

Add potatoes, capers, tomatoes, olives, salt and pepper, stir, cover and cook on High for 7 minutes.

Add pine nuts and raisins, stir again, divide into bowls and serve for breakfast.

Enjoy!

Nutrition: calories 162, fat 3, fiber 4, carbs 7, protein 7

BANANA OATMEAL

Preparation time: 10 minutes

Cooking Time: 10 minutes

Servings: 4

Ingredients:

- 2 cups water
- 1 cup almond milk
- 1 cup steel cut oats
- ¼ cup walnuts, chopped
- 2 tablespoons chia seeds
- 2 tablespoons flaxseed meal
- 1 banana, peeled and mashed
- 1 teaspoon cinnamon powder
- 2 tablespoons maple syrup
- 1 teaspoon vanilla extract

Directions:

1. In your instant pot, mix water with almond milk, oats, walnuts, chia seeds, flaxseed meal, banana, cinnamon, maple syrup and vanilla extract, stir, cover and cook on High for 10 minutes.

2. Stir oatmeal again, divide into bowls and serve for breakfast.

3. Enjoy!

Nutrition: calories 300, fat 12, fiber 10, carbs 28, protein 11

JACKFRUIT BREAKFAST MIX

Preparation time: 10 minutes

Cooking Time: 25 minutes

Servings: 4

Ingredients:

2 bay leaves

- 1 teaspoon olive oil
- ½ teaspoon cumin seeds
- ½ teaspoon mustard seeds
- 2 red chilies, dried
- 1 yellow onion, chopped
- 5 garlic cloves, minced
- ½ teaspoon nigella seeds
- ½ teaspoon turmeric powder
- 1 small ginger piece, grated
- 1 teaspoon coriander powder
- A pinch of salt and black pepper
- 2 tomatoes, pureed
- 20 ounces canned green jackfruit, drained
- 1 and ½ cups water

Directions:

1. Set your instant pot on sauté mode, add oil, heat it up, add cumin, mustard seeds, nigella seeds, chilies and bay leaves, stir and cook for 1 minute.

2. Add ginger, onion, garlic, salt and pepper, stir and cook for 5 minutes

more.

3. Add turmeric, coriander, tomato puree, water and jackfruit, stir, cover and cook on High for 10 minutes.

4. Stir again, divide into bowls and serve.

5. Enjoy!

Nutrition: calories 200, fat 4, fiber 7, carbs 8, protein 12

VEGGIES AND COCONUT SAUCE

Preparation time: 10 minutes

Cooking Time: 20 minutes

Servings: 4

Ingredients:

- 2 teaspoons sesame seeds
- 1 teaspoon coriander seeds
- ½ teaspoon poppy seeds
- ½ teaspoon black peppercorns
- ½ teaspoon mustard seeds
- ½ teaspoon cumin seeds
- ¼ teaspoon fenugreek seeds
- 2 tablespoons coconut, shredded
- 4 red chilies, dried
- ½ teaspoon nutmeg, ground
- ¼ teaspoon cinnamon powder
- ½ teaspoon sweet paprika
- 1 small yellow onion, chopped
- 4 garlic cloves, minced
- 2 tomatoes, chopped
- A pinch of salt and black pepper
- 2 cups cauliflower florets
- 1 and ½ cups sweet potatoes, chopped
- 2 cups carrots, grated
- 2 cups water
- ½ cup red bell pepper, chopped

Directions:

1. Set your instant pot on sauté mode, heat it up, add sesame seeds, coriander seeds, poppy seeds, black peppercorns, mustard seeds, cumin seeds, fenugreek seeds, coconut, chilies, nutmeg, cinnamon and paprika, stir and cook for a couple of minutes.

2. Add onion, garlic, tomatoes, salt and pepper, stir and cook for 2 minutes more.

3. Add cauliflower, carrots, sweet potatoes, red bell pepper and water, stir, cover and cook on High for 15 minutes.

4. Stir everything one more time, divide into bowls and serve for breakfast.

5. Enjoy!

Nutrition: calories 200, fat 5, fiber 5, carbs 7, protein 10

BLACKBERRY OATMEAL

Preparation time: 10 minutes

Cooking Time: 30 minutes

Servings: 6

Ingredients:

- 3 cups water
- 14 ounces coconut milk
- 3 tablespoons stevia

- 2 and ¼ cups steel cut oats
- 1 cup blueberries
- 1 teaspoon vanilla extract
- ¼ cup coconut flour

Directions:

1. In your instant pot, mix water with coconut milk, stevia, steel cut oats, blueberries, vanilla extract and flour, stir, cover and cook on High for 30 minutes.

2. Stir your oatmeal one more time, divide into bowls and serve for breakfast.

3. Enjoy!

Nutrition: calories 300, fat 7, fiber 6, carbs 20, protein 7

BLUEBERRY AND QUINOA BOWL

Preparation time: 10 minutes

Cooking Time: 3 minutes

Servings: 4

Ingredients:

- 1 and ½ cups quinoa
- 1 cinnamon stick
- 1 and ½ cups water
- ¼ cup raisins
- 1 tablespoon stevia
- 1 apple, cored, peeled and grated
- 1 cup natural apple juice
- 1 cup coconut yogurt
- ¼ cup pistachios, chopped
- ¼ cup blueberries

Directions:

1. In your instant pot, mix quinoa with cinnamon and water, stir, cover and cook on High for 3 minutes.

2. Strain, transfer quinoa to a bowl, add stevia, apple, apple juice, yogurt, pistachios and blueberries, toss well and serve cold for breakfast.

3. Enjoy!

Nutrition: calories 200, fat 4, fiber 6, carbs 8, protein 8

40. STRAWBERRY BREAKFAST BOWLS

Preparation time: 10 minutes

Cooking Time: 10 minutes

Servings: 2

Ingredients:

- 1 and ½ cups water
- 1 cup steel cut oats
- 1 cup strawberries, halved
- 2 tablespoons coconut oil
- 1 cup orange juice
- 1 tablespoon cranberries, dried
- 1 tablespoon raisins
- 2 tablespoons maple syrup
- 1 tablespoon apricots, dried and chopped
- 2 tablespoons pecans, chopped
- ¼ teaspoon cinnamon powder

Directions:

1. In your instant pot, mix water with oats, coconut oil, orange juice, cranberries, maple syrup, raisins,

apricots, pecans and cinnamon, stir, cover and cook on High for 10 minutes.

2. Add strawberries, toss your mix, divide into bowls and serve for breakfast.

3. Enjoy!

Nutrition: calories 172, fat 4, fiber 2, carbs 10, protein 5

BREAKFAST PORRIDGE

Preparation time: 10 minutes

Cooking Time: 6 minutes

Servings: 4

Ingredients:

- 1 cup buckwheat
- 3 cups almond milk
- 1 banana, peeled and sliced
- ¼ cup raisins
- ½ teaspoon vanilla extract
- 1 teaspoon cinnamon powder
- 1 tablespoon favorite nuts, chopped

Directions:

1. In your instant pot, mix buckwheat with milk, banana, raisins, vanilla extract and cinnamon, stir, cover and cook on High for 6 minutes.

2. Add nuts, toss, divide into bowls and serve for breakfast.

3. Enjoy!

Nutrition: calories 192, fat 4, fiber 5, carbs 10, protein 8

MUSHROOM PORRIDGE

Preparation time: 10 minutes

Cooking Time: 15 minutes

Servings: 4

Ingredients:

- 2 garlic cloves, minced
- 1 small yellow onion, chopped
- 1 cup steel cut oats
- 14 ounces veggie stock
- 3 thyme sprigs, chopped
- 2 tablespoons olive oil
- A pinch of salt and black pepper
- 8 ounces mushrooms, chopped

Directions:

1. Set your instant pot on sauté mode, add the oil, heat it up, add onion and garlic, stir and cook for 2 minutes.

2. Add mushrooms and thyme, salt and pepper, stir and cook for 3 minutes more.

3. Add oats and stock, stir, cover and cook on High for 10 minutes.

4. Stir porridge one more time, divide into bowls and serve for breakfast.

5. Enjoy!

Nutrition: calories 210, fat 3, fiber 8, carbs 12, protein 17

POPCORN CAULIFLOWER

Preparation Time: 10 minutes

Cooking Time: 7 minutes

Servings: 2

Ingredients:

- ½ cup cauliflower florets
- 1 teaspoon turmeric
- 1 teaspoon curry powder
- ¼ cup wheat flour
- 4 tablespoons coconut cream
- 1 teaspoon salt
- 1 teaspoon chili flakes
- 1 tablespoon bread crumbs
- 1 cup water, for cooking

Directions:

1. In the mixing bowl combine together turmeric, curry powder, wheat flour, coconut cream, salt, and chili flakes.
2. Whisk the mixture well.
3. Then add cauliflower florets and shake. When all the cauliflower florets are coated, sprinkle them with the bread crumbs.
4. Pour water in the instant pot and insert rack.
5. Place cauliflower florets into the instant pot pan.
6. Transfer the pan on the rack. Close and seal the lid.
7. Cook cauliflower popcorn for 7 minutes on manual mode (high pressure)
8. When the time is over, use quick pressure release.
9. Open the lid and chill the meal till the room temperature.

Nutrition Values: Calories 153, fat 7.8, fiber 2.4, carbs 18.7, protein 3.5

LENTIL STEAK

Preparation Time: 10 minutes

Cooking Time: 8 minutes

Servings: 2

Ingredients:

- 1 cup lentils, cooked
- ½ cup bread crumbs
- 3 tablespoons wheat flour
- 1 teaspoon salt
- ½ teaspoon chili pepper
- 1 teaspoon dried oregano
- 1 tablespoon olive oil

Directions:

1. Place lentils into the mixing bowl and mash them with the help of the fork.
2. After this, add wheat flour, salt, chili pepper, and dried oregano.
3. Mix up the mixture until homogenous.
4. With the help of the fingertips make 2 balls and press them to make steak shape.

5. Preheat instant pot on saute mode.

6. Then add olive oil.

7. Coat lentil steaks in bread crumbs.

8. Put the steaks in the preheated olive oil.

9. Cook them for 3 minutes from each side or until they are light brown.

Nutrition Values: Calories 551, fat 9.7, fiber 31.2, carbs 86.7, protein 29.7

RAVIOLI

Preparation Time: 15 minutes

Cooking Time: 10 minutes

Servings: 6

Ingredients:

- 1 cup pumpkin puree
- 3 oz vegan Parmesan, grated
- 1 tablespoon fresh parsley, chopped
- ½ teaspoon ground black pepper
- ½ teaspoon salt
- 1 cup wheat flour
- ¼ cup of water
- 5 tablespoons aquafaba
- 1 cup water, for cooking

Directions:

1. Make the ravioli filling: in the mixing bowl mix up together pumpkin puree, grated Parmesan, chopped parsley, ground black pepper, and salt.

2. Make ravioli dough: mix up together ¼ cup of water, wheat flour, and aquafaba. Knead soft but mom-sticky dough.

3. Roll up the dough with the help of the rolling pin.

4. Then make the ravioli bags with the help of the cutter.

5. Fill the ravioli bags with pumpkin puree filling and secure the edges.

6. Pour 1 cup of water in the instant pot.

7. Add ravioli.

8. Set Saute mode and cook ravioli until they start to boil (approximately for 6-7 minutes).

9. Then close and seal the lid and set Manual mode.

10. Cook ravioli for 3 minutes more.

11. After this, make quick pressure release.

12. Drain water and transfer ravioli into the serving bowls.

Nutrition Values: Calories 134, fat 0.3, fiber 1.8, carbs 22.3, protein 8.4

VEGAN PEPPERONI

Preparation Time: 15 minutes

Cooking Time: 5 minutes

Servings: 4

Ingredients:

- ½ cup wheat flour
- 1 teaspoon salt
- 1 teaspoon paprika
- ½ teaspoon ground cardamom
- 1 teaspoon ground black pepper
- 1 tablespoon tomato paste
- 1 teaspoon soy sauce
- 1 teaspoon olive oil

- 3 tablespoons water
- 1 tablespoon nutritional yeast
- 1 cup water, for cooking

Directions:

1. In the mixing bowl mix up together all the dry ingredients.
2. Then add tomato paste, soy sauce, water, and mix it.
3. When the mixture is homogenous, add olive and knead it
4. Make the log from the pepperoni dough and wrap it into the foil and parchment.
5. Pour 1 cup of water in the instant pot.
6. Insert rack and place pepperoni log on it/
7. Close and seal the lid.
8. Set high-pressure mode (manual) and cook it for 5 minutes.
9. Then allow natural pressure release.
10. Open the instant pot lid, discard foil/parchment from the pepperoni log, slice it and transfer on the serving plate.

Nutrition Values: Calories 83, fat 1.6, fiber 1.6, carbs 14.8, protein 3.2

VEGAN SAUSAGES

Preparation Time: 10 minutes

Cooking Time: 6 minutes

Servings: 2

Ingredients:

- 1 teaspoon olive oil
- 1 small onion, chopped

- ¼ teaspoon garlic, diced
- ½ cup chickpeas, cooked
- 1 teaspoon tomato paste
- 1 teaspoon ground cumin
- ½ teaspoon salt
- 1 teaspoon dried parsley
- ¼ teaspoon ground black pepper
- 4 tablespoons oatmeal flour

Directions:

1. In the food processor, combine together chopped onion, garlic, chickpeas, tomato paste, ground cumin, salt, dried parsley, ground black pepper, and oatmeal flour.
2. Process the mixture until smooth.
3. Then transfer it into the mixing bowl.
4. Preheat instant pot on saute mode.
5. Meanwhile, make the medium size sausages from the chickpea mixture.
6. Pour olive oil in the hot instant pot.
7. Then add prepared sausages and saute them for 2-3 minutes from each side.
8. The cooked sausages should have a light brown color.

Nutrition Values: Calories 254, fat 6.2, fiber 10.7, carbs 40, protein 11.8

DELI SLICES

Preparation Time: 25 minutes

Cooking Time: 17 minutes

Servings: 6

Ingredients:

- 4 oz vegetable stock

- 1 teaspoon tomato paste
- 5 oz firm tofu, chopped
- 7 tablespoons flour
- 2 tablespoons nutritional yeast
- ½ teaspoon minced garlic
- 1 teaspoon paprika
- ½ teaspoon white pepper
- 1 teaspoon coconut oil
- 1 cup water, for cooking

Directions:

1. In the blender combine together tomato paste, firm tofu, nutritional yeast, minced garlic, paprika, vegetable stock, white pepper, and coconut oil.
2. Blend the mixture until smooth.
3. After this, place flour in the mixing bowl.
4. Add blended mixture. Mix up the mass.
5. Wrap the mass into the foil and make the shape of the log.
6. Pour water in the instant pot.
7. Insert steamer rack.
8. Place wrapped log on the steamer. Close and seal the lid.
9. Set Steam mode and cook the meal for 7 minutes. Use natural pressure release for 10 minutes.
10. Discard the foil from the log and chill it for at least 30 minutes.
11. Slice it.

Nutrition Values: Calories 72, fat 2.1, fiber 1.6, carbs 9.6, protein 4.6

MUSHROOM PIE

Preparation Time: 30 minutes

Cooking Time: 30 minutes

Servings: 4

Ingredients:

- 2 cups mushrooms, chopped
- 2 white onions, chopped
- 1 tablespoon coconut oil
- 1 teaspoon salt
- 1 teaspoon ground black pepper
- ½ teaspoon sesame seeds
- 1 teaspoon olive oil
- 7 oz puff pastry
- ½ cup water, for cooking

Directions:

1. Place mushrooms, onions, and coconut oil in the instant pot.
2. Add ground black pepper and salt. Mix up the ingredients and cook them on Saute mode for 15 minutes. Stir them from time to time.
3. After this, transfer the mushroom mixture in the bowl.
4. Clean the instant pot.
5. Pour water inside.
6. Take the non-sticky instant pot springform pan.
7. Cut puff pastry into halves.
8. Roll up the dough halves.
9. Place 1 puff pastry half in the springform pan, add mushroom mixture, and cover it with the second half of puff pastry.
10. Secure the edges with the fork.

11. Brush the surface of the pie with olive oil and sprinkle with sesame seeds. Cover the pie with the foil and pin small holes.

12. Set steamer rack in the instant pot.

13. Place the pan on the rack. Close and seal the lid.

14. Set manual mode (high pressure) and cook pie for 15 minutes.

15. Allow natural pressure release for 10 minutes.

16. Open the lid, remove the pan with pie from it, discard foil.

17. Transfer the pie on the serving plate and cut it into the slices.

Nutrition Values: Calories 346, fat 23.8, fiber 2.5, carbs 29.1, protein 5.5

STUFFED SPINACH SHELLS

Preparation Time: 10 minutes

Cooking Time: 14 minutes

Servings: 2

Ingredients:

- 1 cup pasta shells
- ½ cup tomato sauce
- 2 cup spinach
- 4 oz vegan Parmesan, grated
- 1 teaspoon minced garlic
- ½ teaspoon ground black pepper
- 1 tablespoon olive oil
- ½ onion, diced
- ½ cup of water

Directions:

1. Pour olive oil in the instant pot.

2. Add diced onion and tomato sauce.

3. Then add water and mix the mixture up.

4. Set Saute mode and it for 5 minutes. Stir it from time to time.

5. Meanwhile, chop the spinach and mix it up with minced garlic, ground black pepper, and grated Parmesan.

6. Fill the pasta shells with the spinach mixture.

7. Transfer the filled pasta shells in the instant pot.

8. Close and seal the lid.

9. Set Manual mode (high pressure) and cook the meal for 9 minutes.

10. Then use quick pressure release.

11. Chill the cooked meal little before serving.

Nutrition Values: Calories 620, fat 9.3, fiber 4.3, carbs 94.3, protein 33.3

PUMPKIN RISOTTO

Preparation Time: 10 minutes

Cooking Time: 12 minutes

Servings: 2

Ingredients:

- 1 cup white rice
- 6 tablespoons pumpkin puree
- ½ teaspoon sage
- ½ white onion, diced
- ¼ teaspoon garlic, diced
- 2 cups of water
- 1 teaspoon salt
- 1 teaspoon ground black pepper

- ½ teaspoon paprika
- 1 tablespoon coconut oil

Directions:

1. Place coconut oil in the instant pot and melt it on Saute mode.
2. Add white rice, sage, salt, and ground black pepper.
3. Saute the rice for 3 minutes. Stir it from time to time.
4. After this, add pumpkin puree, diced onion, garlic, paprika, and water.
5. Mix it gently and close the lid.
6. Set Manual mode (high pressure) and cook risotto for 9 minutes.
7. Then use quick pressure release.
8. Open the lid and mix up the meal carefully.

Nutrition Values: Calories 428, fat 7.7, fiber 3.7, carbs 81.4, protein 7.6

STRUDEL

Preparation Time: 10 minutes

Cooking Time: 40 minutes

Servings: 4

Ingredients:

- 1 cup mushrooms, chopped
- 1 onion, diced
- 1 teaspoon olive oil
- 1 teaspoon ground black pepper
- 1 teaspoon salt
- 7 oz puff pastry, vegan
- ½ cup water, for cooking

Directions:

1. On the saute mode, cook together for 10 minutes mushrooms, diced onion, olive oil, salt, and ground black pepper. Mix up the mixture from time to time.
2. Meanwhile, roll up the vegan puff pastry with the help of the rolling pin.
3. Transfer the cooked mushroom mixture over the puff pastry and roll it.
4. Secure the edges of the roll and make the shape of strudel.
5. Pin the strudel with the help of a knife.
6. Then pour water in the instant pot.
7. Place strudel in the non-stick instant pot pan and transfer it in the instant pot. You can use a trivet for instant pot too.
8. Close and seal the lid.
9. Cook the strudel on High pressure (manual mode) for 30 minutes.
10. Then use quick pressure release.
11. Chill the strudel till the room temperature and slice it.

Nutrition Values: Calories 299, fat 20.2, fiber 1.7, carbs 25.9, protein 4.5

TEMPEH RIBS

Preparation Time: 10 minutes

Cooking Time: 6 minutes

Servings: 4

Ingredients:

- 15 oz tempeh
- 1 teaspoon ground black pepper
- 1 teaspoon paprika

- 1 teaspoon turmeric
- 1 teaspoon chili flaked
- 1 teaspoon salt
- ½ teaspoon sugar
- ½ teaspoon garlic powder
- ½ teaspoon onion powder
- 2 tablespoons BBQ sauce
- 1 tablespoon lemon juice
- 1 teaspoon olive oil
- 1 tablespoon chives, for garnish

Directions:

1. Cut tempeh into the wedges.
2. In the mixing bowl, mix up together paprika, ground black pepper, turmeric, chili flakes, salt, sugar, garlic powder, onion powder, BBQ sauce, and lemon juice.
3. Then rub tempeh wedges with the spice mixture generously.
4. Preheat instant pot on Saute mode.
5. When it is hot, add olive oil and tempeh wedges.
6. Cook them for 3 minutes from each side. The cooked meal should have a light brown color.
7. Then transfer the cooked tempeh ribs onto the serving plate and sprinkle with chives.

Nutrition Values: Calories 237, fat 12.9, fiber 0.6, carbs 14.9, protein 20

RAINBOW VEGETABLE PIE

Preparation Time: 15 minutes

Cooking Time: 30 minutes

Servings: 6

Ingredients:

- ¼ cup olive oil
- 1 cup wheat flour
- ¼ cup of water
- 1 teaspoon salt
- 1 zucchini, sliced
- 1 tomato, sliced
- 1 red onion, sliced
- 1 carrot, sliced
- 1 teaspoon coconut oil
- 1 teaspoon ground black pepper
- 1 teaspoon paprika
- 1 teaspoon Italian seasoning
- 1 cup water, for cooking

Directions:

1. Make the dough: mix up together water, oil, and wheat flour. Add salt and knead the non-sticky, soft dough.
2. Cut the dough into 2 parts.
3. Roll up the fist dough part and place it in the pie pan.
4. Then place all vegetables one by one to make the rainbow circle.
5. Sprinkle the pie with coconut oil, ground black pepper, paprika, and Italian seasoning.
6. Roll up the remaining dough and cover vegetables with it.
7. Secure the edges of the pie with the help of the fork.
8. Pour water in the instant pot and insert trivet.
9. Cover the pie with foil and transfer on the trivet.

10. Close and seal the lid.

11. Cook pie for 30 minutes on Manual mode.

12. Then use quick pressure release.

13. Discard foil from the pie and let it chill for 10 minutes.

14. Then transfer pie on the serving plate and slice.

Nutrition Values: Calories 177, fat 9.8, fiber 1.9, carbs 20.6, protein 3

STUFFED MINI PUMPKINS

Preparation Time: 30 minutes

Cooking Time: 60 minutes

Servings: 4

Ingredients:

- 2 mini pumpkin squash, trimmed, cleaned from flesh and seeds

- ½ cup chickpeas, canned

- 1 teaspoon tomato paste

- 1 cup of rice, cooked

- ½ cup fresh parsley, chopped

- 2 tablespoons almond yogurt

- 1 teaspoon chili flakes

- 1 teaspoon salt

- 1 teaspoon peanuts, chopped

- 1 teaspoon olive oil

Directions:

1. In the mixing bowl combine together tomato paste and almond yogurt. Whisk the mixture.

2. Add chili flakes, salt, peanuts, rice, parsley, and chickpeas. Mix up the mixture well.

3. Fill the pumpkins with rice mixture. Add olive oil and wrap them into the foil.

4. Place the mini pumpkins in the instant pot.

5. Close and seal the lid.

6. Set Manual mode (high pressure) and cook a meal for 60 minutes.

7. Then allow natural pressure release for 20 minutes more.

8. Open the lid, discard foil from the pumpkins and transfer meal on the serving plates.

Nutrition Values: Calories 511, fat 4.1, fiber 6.3, carbs 41.7, protein 10.8

NUT LOAF

Preparation Time: 15 minutes

Cooking Time: 20 minutes

Servings: 8

Ingredients:

- 1 teaspoon coconut oil

- 1 teaspoon avocado oil

- 3 oz yellow onion, diced

- 3 oz celery stalk, chopped

- 1 teaspoon garlic, diced

- 1 cup mushrooms, chopped

- ½ jalapeno pepper, chopped

- 3 oz carrot, grated

- 1 cup walnuts, chopped

- ½ cup lentils, cooked

- 1 teaspoon salt

- 1 teaspoon flax meal

- 2 tablespoons water
- ½ cup wheat flour
- 1 tablespoon Italian seasoning
- 1 cup water, for cooking

Directions:

1. Preheat instant pot onsaute mode.
2. When it is hot, add avocado oil, diced onion, and mushrooms.
3. Cook the vegetables for 5 minutes, stir them from time to time.
4. Then add a chopped celery stalk and mix up. Cook the mixture for 5 minutes more.
5. Transfer the cooked vegetables into the mixing bowl.
6. Add coconut oil, jalapeno pepper, grated carrot, walnuts, lentils, salt, and flour. Mix it up.
7. In the separated bowl, mix up together flax meal and 2 tablespoons of water. The egg substitutor is cooked.
8. Add the flax meal mixture into the lentils mixture.
9. Then add Italian seasoning and mix up carefully. In the end, you should get soft but a homogenous mixture. Add more wheat flour if needed.
10. Place the loaf mixture in the boiling bag and seal it.
11. Pour water in the instant pot. Add sealed loaf.
12. Close and seal the instant pot lid.
13. Set Manual mode (high pressure) and cook loaf for 6 minutes. Then allow natural pressure release for 10 minutes more.
14. Remove the boiling bag from the instant pot and take loaf.
15. Chill the loaf for 1-2 hours and only after this, slice it.

Nutrition Values: Calories 193, fat 9.8, fiber 5.8, carbs 17.8, protein 8.3

FRAGRANT SPRING ONIONS

Preparation Time: 15 minutes

Cooking Time: 5 minutes

Servings: 4

Ingredients:

- 1-pound spring onions
- 1 tablespoon avocado oil
- ½ teaspoon ground cumin
- 1 teaspoon dried cilantro
- ½ teaspoon salt
- 1 tablespoon lemon juice

Directions:

1. Wash and trim the spring onions. Then cut them lengthwise.
2. Sprinkle them with the dried cilantro, cumin, salt, and lemon juice.
3. Shake well and leave for 10 minutes to marinate.
4. Meanwhile, preheat instant pot on saute mode until hot.
5. Add avocado oil.
6. After this, add spring onions and cook them on Saute mode for 2 minutes from each side.
7. Then sprinkle the vegetables with remaining lemon juice marinade and cook for 1 minute more. The spring onions are cooked when the tender

but not soft.

Nutrition Values: Calories 43, fat 0.8, fiber 3.2, carbs 8.7, protein 2.2

BEET STEAKS

Preparation Time: 10 minutes

Cooking Time: 27 minutes

Servings: 2

Ingredients:

- 2 red beets, peeled
- 1 portobello mushroom, chopped
- 1 white onion, sliced
- 1 teaspoon thyme
- 1 teaspoon olive oil
- 2 tablespoons red wine

Directions:

1. Slice every beet onto 4 slices.
2. Then sprinkle every beet slice with thyme.
3. Preheat instant pot well and pour olive oil inside.
4. Set Saute mode, add mushrooms and sliced onion. Saute the vegetables for 3 minutes. Stir them from time to time.
5. Transfer the cooked vegetables into the mixing bowl.
6. Then add sliced beets in the instant pot.
7. Add red wine and close the lid.
8. Saute the steaks for 15 minutes.
9. After this, add mushrooms and onion. Mix up the ingredients gently.
10. Close the lid and cook for 10 minutes

more.

11. When the time is over, switch off the instant pot and open the lid.
12. Transfer the cooked beet steaks on the plates and top with the mushroom and wine sauce.

Nutrition Values: Calories 110, fat 2.6, fiber 3.9, carbs 17.3, protein 3.9

STUFFED FIGS

Preparation Time: 10 minutes

Cooking Time: 2 minutes

Servings: 4

Ingredients:

- 4 figs
- ½ teaspoon brown sugar
- 3 tablespoons water
- ¼ teaspoon ground cinnamon
- 4 teaspoons cashew butter
- 1 pinch ground cardamom
- ½ cup water, for cooking

Directions:

1. Crosscut the figs and remove a small amount of fig flesh.
2. Then mix up together cashew butter, ground cinnamon, and ground cardamom.
3. Fill the figs with the cashew butter mixture.
4. Then place them in the instant pot pan.
5. Sprinkle the figs with water and sugar.
6. Pour ½ cup of water in the instant pot and insert trivet.

7. Place pan with figs on the trivet.

8. Close and seal the lid.

9. Set Manual mode (high pressure) and cook figs for 2 minutes. Then use quick pressure release.

10. Open the lid and pour the figs with the sweet juice from them.

11. The main dish should be served hot or warm.

Nutrition Values: Calories 81, fat 2.8, fiber 2.1, carbs 14.1, protein 1.6

SLOPPY JOE IN INSTANT POT

Preparation Time: 35 Minutes

Servings: 6-8

Ingredients:

- 1 cup of red lentils
- 1 rib of celery, chopped
- 1 yellow onion, chopped
- 1/2 of a yellow pepper, chopped
- 1/2 can (1/2 of an 8 oz can) of tomato paste
- 2 1/2 cups of water
- 1/4 cup of red wine vinegar
- 2 tbsp of brown sugar
- 1 tsp of salt
- 1 tsp of liquid smoke
- 3 garlic cloves, minced
- 2 tbsp of sriracha (optional)
- 1/4 cup of oil-free breadcrumbs
- 6 or 8 oil-free hamburger buns

Directions:

1. Except for breadcrumbs and buns, combine all ingredients in Instant Pot. Set steam release handle to 'sealing' and switch on manual button. Cover the pot with lid and set to 15 minutes over high pressure.

2. Allow the pressure to release naturally for 10-15 minutes. Change steam release handle to 'venting' to release extra steam. Open the lid. Add breadcrumbs and give it a stir.

3. Serve this sloppy Joe mix over hamburger buns topped with fresh mixed greens, if desired.

PIZZA ALLAPUTTANESCA.

Preparation Time: 15 Minutes

Servings: 6

Ingredients:

Dough:

- 1½ cups unbleached all-purpose flour
- ½ cup warm water, or as needed
- 1 tablespoon olive oil
- 1½ teaspoons instant yeast
- ½ teaspoon salt
- ½ teaspoon Italian seasoning

Sauce:

- ½ cup crushed tomatoes
- ½ cup shredded vegan mozzarella cheese
- ¼ cup pitted green olives, sliced
- ¼ cup pitted kalamata olives, sliced
- 1 tablespoon chopped fresh flat-leaf parsley
- 1 tablespoon capers, rinsed and drained

- ¼ teaspoon garlic powder
- ¼ teaspoon sugar
- ¼ teaspoon dried basil
- ¼ teaspoon dried oregano
- ¼ teaspoon hot red pepper flakes
- Salt and freshly ground black pepper

Directions:

1. Get a bowl to mix your dough. Whisk together the flour, yeast, salt, and seasoning.
2. Add the oil slowly whilst stirring, then add water little by little until the dough ball is formed.
3. Knead the dough on a floured surface for 2 minutes.
4. Shape it and put it in a warm bowl to rise for an hour.
5. Whilst the dough rises, mix the sauce. Combine tomatoes, olives, capers, parsley, basil, oregano, garlic powder, sugar, red pepper, salt and pepper.
6. Oil a tray that will fit in your instant pot and stretch the dough to fit it.
7. Spread the sauce over the dough.
8. Insert the tray into your instant pot and cook for 10 minutes on steam.
9. Release the pressure quickly and sprinkle the mozzarella on top at the end.

SEITAN FAJITAS.

Preparation Time: 40 Minutes

Servings: 6

Ingredients:

- 1lb seitan, cut into strips

- 2 tablespoons tomato paste
- 1½ cups tomato salsa
- 1 tablespoon chili powder
- 1 tablespoon soy sauce
- 2 large bell peppers (any color), seeded and cut into ¼-inch-thick strips
- 1 large yellow onion, thinly sliced
- 1 garlic clove, minced
- Salt and freshly ground black pepper
- 2 tablespoons freshly squeezed lime juice
- 1 ripe Hass avocado, peeled, pitted, and diced, for garnish
- 1 large ripe tomato, diced, for garnish

Directions:

1. Mix the tomato paste, salsa, chili powder, and soy sauce until combined well.
2. Put the bell peppers, onion, and garlic in your instant pot.
3. Put your seitan strips on top. Try and avoid them touching.
4. Pour the tomato mix over everything.
5. Seal and cook on Poultry for 30 minutes.
6. Depressurize naturally, stir in the lime to taste.
7. Serve and top with avocado and tomato.

ZESTY STUFFED BELL PEPPERS.

Preparation Time: 30 Minutes

Servings: 4

Ingredients:

- 4 large bell peppers (any color or a combination)
- 1 (14-ounce) can tomato sauce
- 2 cups cooked brown or white rice
- 1½ cups cooked pinto beans or black beans or 1 (15-ounce) can beans, rinsed and drained
- 1 cup fresh or thawed frozen corn kernels
- 1 cup diced fresh tomatoes or 1 (14-ounce) can diced tomatoes, drained
- 2 teaspoons olive oil (optional)
- 4 garlic cloves, minced
- 4 scallions, chopped
- 1 tablespoon chili powder
- 2 teaspoons minced chipotle chiles in adobo
- 1½ teaspoon ground cumin
- 1¼ teaspoon dried oregano
- ½ teaspoon sugar
- Salt and freshly ground black pepper

Directions:

1. Warm the oil in your instant pot, leaving the lid open.
2. When the oil is hot, add the garlic and scallions and soften for 3 minutes.
3. Add the chili powder, and a teaspoon of both the cumin and the oregano.
4. Put the garlic mixture in a bowl to one side. Add the rice, beans, corn, tomatoes, and chiles with a little salt and pepper. Mix well.
5. Top and hollow your bell peppers.

6. Fill the peppers evenly with the mix and set them in the steamer basket of your instant pot.
7. Mix the tomato sauce, remaining cumin, remaining oregano, sugar, and salt in the base of your instant pot.
8. Lower the steamer basket, seal, and cook on Steam for 24 minutes.
9. Depressurize fast and serve immediately.

MOROCCAN STUFFED PEPPERS

Preparation Time: 30 Minutes

Servings: 4

Ingredients:

- 4 large bell peppers (assorted colors look great)
- 2 cups boiling water or vegetable broth
- 2 cups couscous
- 1 cup cooked chickpeas or 1 (15-ounce) can chickpeas
- 1 medium-size yellow onion, minced
- 2 carrots, peeled and minced
- 1 large zucchini, minced
- 3 garlic cloves, minced
- 3 tablespoons tomato paste
- 2 teaspoons olive oil
- 2 teaspoons harissa or hot chili paste
- 2 teaspoons ground coriander
- 1 teaspoon paprika
- 1 teaspoon ground cinnamon
- ½ tablespoon ground cumin
- 1 teaspoon salt

- ¼ teaspoon freshly ground black pepper
- 1 tablespoon minced fresh flat-leaf parsley leaves, for garnish

Directions:

1. Top and hollow our the peppers. Remove the stems, then chop the tops and keep the diced pepper.
2. Warm the oil in your instant pot.
3. When hot, add the onion and soften for 4 minutes.
4. Add the carrots, pepper tops, zucchini, garlic, and cook for 2 more minutes.
5. Add the harissa, tomato paste, coriander, cinnamon, cumin, paprika, salt and pepper.
6. Add the couscous and water, stir well.
7. Add the chickpeas and stir again.
8. Pack the stuffing into the peppers and put them in the steamer basket of your instant pot.
9. Put a cup of water in your instant pot. Lower the steamer basket.
10. Seal and cook on Steam for 24 minutes.
11. Depressurize naturally and serve immediately, topped with parsley.

CORN CHORIZO PIE

Preparation Time: 6 Minutes

Servings: 6

Ingredients:

- 12 soft corn tortillas
- 1 crumbled vegan chorizo
- 1 onion, minced

- 1 teaspoon olive oil
- 2canned chipotle chilies in adobo, minced
- 1½cups corn kernels
- 1½cups shredded vegan cheddar cheese
- 2tablespoons chili powder
- 1tablespoon tomato paste
- 1tablespoon grated unsweetened dark chocolate
- 1(15-ounce) can vegan refried beans, stirred
- 1teaspoon ground cumin
- ¼teaspoon black pepper
- 1teaspoon smoked paprika
- 1teaspoon dark brown sugar
- 1teaspoon dried oregano
- 8ounces steamed diced tempeh, chopped seitan
- ½teaspoon salt
- 1(14.5-ounce) can crushed tomatoes
- 4garlic cloves, minced
- 1½cups cooked pinto beans

Directions:

1. Add the onion, garlic and oil in the instant pot.
2. Cook for 30 seconds and then add the tomato paste, cumin, chipotle chiles, chocolate, oregano, chili powder, paprika, brown sugar, and seasoning.
3. Add some water and cover with lid.
4. Cook for 2 minutes and then add the tomatoes.

5. Cover and cook for 1 minute.

6. Add the tempeh, beans, corn and mix well.

7. Cover and cook for another 5 minutes.

8. Serve hot.

CHEESY TOMATO GRATIN

Preparation Time: 10 Minutes

Servings: 6

Ingredients:

- 1(14.5-ounce) can petite diced tomatoes
- 1cup shredded vegan mozzarella cheese
- 3large potatoes, peeled and sliced
- ½teaspoon smoked paprika
- ¼cup vegetable broth
- 1onion, minced
- 2tablespoons chili powder
- ½teaspoon ground cumin
- ¼teaspoon cayenne pepper
- 3garlic cloves, minced
- 1teaspoon dried oregano
- 3tablespoons tomato paste
- Salt and black pepper

Directions:

1. Add the onion, garlic in your instant pot.

2. Cover and cook for 30 seconds.

3. Add the broth, oregano, cumin, tomato paste, cayenne, paprika and chili powder.

4. Add the tomatoes, and mix well.

5. Cook for 2 minutes.

6. Add the potato slices and cook for 4 minutes.

7. Add the cheese and cook for another minute.

8. Serve warm.

SWEET POTATOES AND ONIONS WITH JERK SAUCE

Preparation Time: 6 Minutes

Servings: 6

Ingredients:

- 2sweet potatoes, peeled and diced
- 1pound tempeh, diced
- ½ sweet onion, diced
- ¼teaspoon cayenne pepper
- 1garlic clove, crushed
- ¼teaspoon paprika
- 2scallions, coarsely chopped
- 2teaspoons soy sauce
- 1tablespoon ginger
- 2tablespoons lime
- 1teaspoon dried thyme
- 1teaspoon dark brown sugar
- 1hot green chile, seeded and chopped
- ½teaspoon ground allspice
- ¼teaspoon ground cinnamon
- ½teaspoon salt
- 1tablespoon rice vinegar
- ¼teaspoon black pepper
- ⅓cup water

- ½ large or 1 small Vidalia or other sweet onion, cut into ½-inch dice

Directions:

1. In a blender add the chile, scallions, ginger, garlic and onion.
2. Blend for 30 seconds and add the soy sauce, cinnamon, cayenne, seasoning, vinegar, marmalade, allspice, sugar and thyme.
3. Add some water and blend again.
4. Add the tempeh, onion and potatoes in the instant pot.
5. Add the jerk sauce you made.
6. Mix well and cook for 5 minutes.
7. Serve warm.

ZITI MUSHROOM STEW

Preparation Time: 6 Minutes

Servings: 4

Ingredients:

- 1 bell pepper, seeded and minced
- 1 onion, minced
- 1 (14-ounce) can crushed tomatoes
- 4 garlic cloves, minced
- 2 tablespoons tomato paste
- ½ cup dry red wine
- 8 ounces white mushrooms, coarsely chopped
- 1 cup hot water
- 8 ounces uncooked ziti
- 1 teaspoon dried basil
- Salt and black pepper
- 2 teaspoons minced fresh oregano

- 1 teaspoon natural sugar
- 2 tablespoons chopped parsley

Directions:

1. Add the ziti, mushroom, red wine, tomato paste in an instant pot.
2. Add the sugar, herbs, spices, hot water and the rest of the ingredients.
3. Mix well and cook for 5 minutes with the lid on.
4. Serve hot.

TOFU CHEESECAKE

Preparation Time: 15 Minutes

Servings: 8-12

Ingredients:

- 8 ounces silken tofu
- ¼ cup dried bread crumbs
- 3 garlic cloves, crushed
- 1 teaspoon salt
- 1 cup raw cashews, soaked
- 2 tablespoons sun-dried tomatoes, chopped
- 1 cup vegan cream cheese
- 2 tablespoons parsley, minced
- 2 tablespoons pitted olives, chopped
- ¼ teaspoon cayenne pepper
- 2 tablespoons minced fresh basil
- 1 tablespoon cornstarch
- 1 teaspoon minced oregano

Directions:

1. Combine the parsley, basil, and tomatoes in a bowl. Mix well and set

aside for now.

2. Add the breadcrumbs onto a baking pan and use hands to make the top even.

3. Add the cashew, salt and garlic in a blender. Blend until smooth.

4. Add the tofu, cream cheese and blend again.

5. Add tomatoes, oregano, olives, cayenne, basil, cornstarch, and blend again.

6. Add on top of the crust.

7. Use aluminum foil to cover the top. Make some holes.

8. Add to your instant pot and cook for about 8 minutes.

9. Serve cold with the cherry tomato mix on top.

GARLIC PIMENTO FONDUE

Preparation Time: 15 Minutes

Servings: 4

Ingredients:

- 1 can white beans, drained and rinsed
- 2 cups shredded vegan cheddar cheese
- 1 jar diced pimentos, drained
- 1/2 teaspoon Dijon mustard
- 1 clove garlic, minced
- 2 tablespoons vegan chicken-flavored bouillon
- 2 tablespoons olive oil
- 1/4 teaspoon salt
- 1/4 teaspoon pepper
- 3/4 cup water

Directions:

1. Process the beans and water in a food processor until pureed.

2. Spray the instant pot with nonstick spray and the pureed beans and everything but the cheese. Seal the lid and cook on high 4 minutes, then let the pressure release naturally. Remove the lid and stir in the cheese. Serve in a fondue pot to keep warm.

SWEET AND NUTTY FONDUE

Preparation Time: 15 Minutes

Servings: 4

Ingredients:

- 1/2 cup almond butter
- 1/2 tablespoons grated ginger
- 1 can coconut milk
- 1 teaspoon soy sauce
- 1 clove garlic, minced
- 1/4 teaspoon chili powder
- 1/4 teaspoon cayenne pepper
- 1/2 teaspoon garam masala
- 1 tablespoon cornstarch, if needed

Directions:

1. Spray the instant pot with nonstick spray.

2. Stir together all the ingredients except for the cornstarch and add them to the instant pot. Seal the lid and cook on high 4 minutes. Quick release the pressure.

3. Remove the lid and check the consistency. If it needs to be thickened, switch to the sauté setting of the instant pot, add the cornstarch,

and cook for 15 minutes.

BEEFY CAJUN PO BOY

Preparation Time: 35 Minutes

Servings: 4

Ingredients:

- 3 cups cubed beef-flavored seitan, thinly sliced
- 2 cloves garlic, minced
- 1 tablespoon vegan Worcestershire sauce
- 2 tablespoons vegan beef-flavored bouillon
- 1/2 teaspoon Cajun seasoning
- 1/4 teaspoon pepper
- 1 bay leaf
- 1 tablespoons cornstarch
- 1 1/2 cups water
- French bread, for serving
- Lettuce, for serving
- Tomato, for serving
- Vegan Mayonnaise, for serving.

Directions:

1. Mix together the garlic, water, Worcestershire sauce, Cajun seasoning, bouillon, water, and bay leaf in the instant pot.

2. Add the sliced seitan. Seal the lid and cook on high 4 minutes. Let pressure release naturally, then remove the lid and the bay leaf.

3. Return to sauté setting and add the cornstarch. Cook an additional 20 minutes, adding additional cornstarch

if needed.

4. Serve on French bread, topped with lettuce, tomato, and vegan mayonnaise.

MEATLESS PHILLY CHEESESTEAK HOAGIE

Preparation Time: 30 Minutes

Servings: 6

Ingredients:

- 4 large Portobello mushrooms, sliced
- 2 large bell peppers, cut into strips
- 1 onion, halved and sliced
- 2 tablespoons vegan beef-flavored bouillon
- 1 tablespoon vegan Worcestershire sauce
- 1 tablespoon cornstarch
- 1/2 cup water
- 6 hoagie rolls, for serving
- Shredded vegan cheddar cheese, for serving

Directions:

1. Combine all the ingredients in the instant pot. Seal the lid and cook on high 3 minutes, then let the pressure release naturally.

2. Switch to sauté setting and add the cornstarch. Simmer for 20 minutes, until gravy is thickened.

3. Serve on a toasted hoagie roll topped with shredded cheese.

SLOPPY TEMPEH SANDWICH

Preparation Time: 25 Minutes

Servings: 6

Ingredients:

- 16 ounces tempeh, cubed
- 1 tablespoon tomato paste
- 1 onion, diced
- 3 cloves garlic
- 1/2 bell pepper, chopped
- 1 can diced tomatoes
- 1/4 cup water
- 1 tablespoon maple syrup
- 1 teaspoon vegan Worcestershire sauce
- 1 tablespoon apple cider vinegar
- 1/2 teaspoon smoked paprika
- 1/2 teaspoon chipotle chili powder
- 1/2 teaspoon cumin
- 1/2 teaspoon chili powder
- 1/4 teaspoon hot sauce
- 1/2 teaspoon salt
- 1 teaspoon Dijon
- 12 buns, for serving

Directions:

1. Use a steamer basket to steam the tempeh for 10 minutes.

2. Heat the oil in the instant pot on the sauté setting and cook the onion for 5 minutes. Add the garlic and peppers and cook an additional 5 minutes.

3. Add the rest of the ingredients to the instant pot, seal the lid, and cook on high 4 minutes. Let the pressure release naturally, then remove the lid and serve on buns.

TEX MEX TOFU TACO 'MEAT'

Preparation Time: 20 Minutes

Servings: 6

Ingredients:

- 15 ounces firm tofu, cubed
- 1 clove garlic, minced
- 1/2 teaspoon chili powder
- 3 tablespoons salsa
- 1/4 teaspoon cumin
- 1/8 teaspoon cayenne pepper
- 1/2 teaspoon fresh ground pepper
- 1/4 teaspoon smoked paprika
- 1/4 teaspoon salt
- Zest of 1 lime
- Juice of 1 lime
- Taco shells, for serving

Directions:

1. Spray the instant pot with nonstick spray. Combine all the ingredients and cook on high 4 minutes.

2. Let the pressure release naturally, then remove the lid. If the sauce is too thin, switch to sauté setting and cook for 5 to 10 minutes to reduce the sauce.

3. Serve on taco shells with your favorite toppings, or use as a taco salad topping.

BLACK BEAN AND POTATO BURRITO FILLING

Preparation Time: 20 Minutes

Servings: 6

Ingredients:

- 4 large russet potatoes, peeled and chopped
- 8 ounces corn
- 1/2 bell pepper, chopped
- 8 ounces black beans
- 1 cup water
- 1 1/2 cups salsa
- 1/4 teaspoon chili powder
- 1/4 teaspoon salt
- Tortillas, for serving

Directions:

1. Spray the instant pot with nonstick spray.
2. Add all the ingredients. Seal the lid and cook on high 4 minutes. Let the pressure release naturally.
3. Use an immersion blender to puree the mixture. Add additional salt if needed and serve wrapped in warm tortillas.

PESTO BUTTERNUT GRILLED SANDWICHES

Preparation Time: 25 Minutes

Servings: 6

Ingredients:

- 1 butternut squash, halved
- 1 teaspoon ground sage
- 4 fresh rosemary leaves
- 1/2 teaspoon ground thyme
- 5 fresh basil leaves
- 1/2 cup walnuts
- 2 tablespoons olive oil
- 1/4 cup nutritional yeast
- 12 slices bread, for serving

Directions:

1. Combine seasonings, herbs, walnuts, and olive oil in a food processor and blend to make the pesto. Set aside.
2. Find a butternut squash that will fit into your instant pot and cut it in half. Remove the seeds and place squash in an oiled instant pot.
3. Seal the lid and cook on high for 6 minutes, then let pressure release naturally.
4. Remove the lid and allow the squash to cool.
5. Scoop out the flesh from the squash. You will use about 2 cups.
6. Mix the squash with the pesto and the yeast.
7. To serve, spread the mixture on bread. Top with another piece of bread and grill in a hot, oiled skillet.

SOY GINGER LETTUCE WRAPS

Preparation Time: 25 Minutes

Servings: 6

Ingredients:

- 8 ounces tempeh cubed
- 1 large stalk celery
- 2 carrots, chopped
- 1 can water chestnuts, drained
- 1 jalapeno, diced
- 2 cloves garlic, minced
- 1 tablespoon grated ginger

- 1 1/4 cups water
- 1/4 cup soy sauce
- 1/4 cup rice vinegar
- 1 teaspoon sugar
- 1/4 teaspoon red pepper flakes
- 1/2 teaspoon sesame seeds
- Whole butter lettuce leaves, for serving
- Cooked rice, for serving

Directions:

1. Use a steamer basket to steam the tempeh for 10 minutes.
2. Mix together the rest of the ingredients in a medium-sized bowl to make the ginger sauce.
3. Add all the ingredients to the instant pot and cook on high 4 minutes. Let the pressure release naturally before removing the lid.
4. Place a small scoop of rice into each lettuce leaf, then add tempeh mixture to each leaf and serve.

QUINOA PECAN STUFFED SQUASH

Preparation Time: 20 Minutes

Servings: 2

Ingredients:

- 1 small acorn squash, halved and seeded
- 1 tablespoon chopped dried cranberries
- 1 can kidney beans, drained and rinsed
- 1 tablespoon chopped pecans

- 1 cup cooked quinoa
- 1 clove garlic, minced
- 1 teaspoon thyme, minced
- Salt and pepper, to taste
- 1/4 cup white wine
- Water

Directions:

1. Mix together the rice, pecans, garlic, thyme, kidney beans, cranberries, salt, and pepper. Add white wine to moisten the mixture.
2. Fill each squash half with the stuffing mixture.
3. Spray the instant pot with nonstick spray. Place the squash halves into the instant pot. If they do not both fit in the bottom, place foil on top of one and place the other on top, making sure they stay below the fill line. You may need to cook each half separately if the halves are too large.
4. Seal the lid and cook on high 6 minutes, then release pressure naturally and serve.

SIDES

BUTTERY STEAMED SWEET POTATOES

Preparation Time: 35 minutes

Servings 4

Nutrition Values: 154 Calories; 5.9g Fat; 23.5g Carbs; 2.3g Protein; 7.3g Sugars

Ingredients

- 1 pound whole small sweet potatoes, cleaned
- 1/4 teaspoon salt
- 1/4 teaspoon freshly grated nutmeg
- 2 tablespoons light butter

Directions

1. Add 1 cup of water and a steamer basket to the Instant Pot. Arrange sweet potatoes in the steamer basket.

2. Secure the lid and choose the "Steam" mode. Cook for 10 minutes under High pressure. Once cooking is complete, use a natural release for 20 minutes; carefully remove the lid.

3. Toss steamed sweet potatoes with salt, nutmeg and butter. Eat warm. Bon appétit!

ARTICHOKES WITH AVOCADO FETA DIP

Preparation Time: 20 minutes

Servings 3

Nutrition Values: 282 Calories; 17.7g Fat; 26.3g Carbs; 10.9g Protein; 4.2g Sugars

Ingredients

- 1 cup water
- 3 globe artichokes
- 1/2 lemon
- For the Sauce:
- 1 avocado, peeled, pitted and diced
- 3 ounces feta cheese
- 1/2 lemon, juiced
- 1/2 yellow onion, chopped
- 2 tablespoons fresh parsley leaves, chopped
- 1/2 teaspoon sea salt
- 1/3 teaspoon black pepper

Directions

1. Add 1 cup of water and a steamer basket to the base of your Instant Pot. Now, discard the damaged leaves of the artichokes.

2. Cut the bottoms to be flat. Cut off excess stem and remove the tough ends of the leaves; rub with a lemon half.

3. Arrange the artichokes in the steamer basket.

4. Secure the lid. Choose the "Manual" mode, High pressure and 11 minutes. Once cooking is complete, use a natural release; carefully remove the lid.

5. In a mixing bowl, combine all the sauce ingredients. Serve the artichokes with the sauce on the

side.Bon appétit!

MOONG DAL AND GREEN BEAN SOUP

Preparation Time: 45 minutes

Servings 6

Nutrition Values: 221 Calories; 4.3g Fat; 34.7g Carbs; 12.8g Protein; 2.1g Sugars

Ingredients

- 1 ½ tablespoons olive oil
- 2 shallots, chopped
- 2 garlic cloves, minced
- 1 teaspoon cilantro, ground
- 1/2 teaspoon ground allspice
- 1/2 teaspoon smoked paprika
- 1 teaspoon celery seeds
- 1/2 teaspoon fennel seeds
- 1/2 teaspoon ground cumin
- 1 ½ cups moong dal
- 7 cups water
- Sea salt and ground black pepper, to your liking
- 2 cups green beans, fresh

Directions

1. Press the "Sauté" button to heat up your Instant Pot. Then, heat olive oil and cook the shallots until just tender.

2. Now, add garlic and cook 30 to 40 seconds more or until it is aromatic and slightly browned. Stir in all seasonings; cook until aromatic or 2 minutes more, stirring continuously.

3. Add the moong dal and water. Secure the lid. Select the "Manual" mode and cook for 17 minutes under High pressure.

4. Once cooking is complete, use a natural pressure release for 20 minutes; carefully remove the lid.

5. Season with sea salt and black pepper; add green beans and secure the lid again. Select the "Manual" mode one more time and cook for 2 minutes under High pressure.

6. Once cooking is complete, use a quick pressure release; carefully remove the lid. Serve immediately with garlic croutons. Bon appétit!

FRENCH-STYLE ONION SOUP

Preparation Time: 35 minutes

Servings 6

Nutrition Values: 353 Calories; 15.4g Fat; 40.5g Carbs; 15.4g Protein; 20.2g Sugars

Ingredients

- 3 tablespoons ghee
- 6 sweet onions, sliced
- 2 garlic cloves
- Kosher salt and ground black pepper, to taste
- 1/2 teaspoon cayenne pepper
- 1 tablespoon granulated sugar
- 1/3 cup sherry wine
- 1/2 cup water
- 5 cups chicken stock, preferably homemade
- 2 fresh rosemary sprigs
- 1 loaf French bread, cut into slices

- and toasted
- 1 ½ cups Munster cheese,shaved

Directions

1. Press the "Sauté" button to heat up the Instant Pot. Then, melt the ghee; sauté the onions until translucent, about 5 minutes.

2. Add garlic and sauté it for 1 to 2 minutes more. Reduce the heat to low; add the salt, black pepper, cayenne pepper, and white sugar. Continue to cook, stirring frequently, until sweet onions are slightly browned.

3. Pour in sherry wine, and scrape off any brown bits from the bottom of your Instant Pot. Now, pour in the water and chicken stock; add rosemary and stir to combine.

4. Secure the lid. Select the "Manual" setting; cook for 8 minutesunder High pressure. Once cooking is complete, use a quick pressure release; carefully remove the lid.

5. Then, preheat your oven to broil.

6. Divide the soup among ovenproof bowls; top with toasted bread and shaved Munster cheese; place your soup under the broiler for 5 to 6 minutes, or until the cheese is bubbly.Serve warm and enjoy!

MASHED POTATOES WITH SPRING GARLIC AND SOUR CREAM

Preparation Time: 15 minutes

Servings 4

Nutrition Values: 230 Calories; 14g Fat; 23.3g Carbs; 3.8g Protein; 1.7g Sugars

Ingredients

- 1 cup water
- 1 pound Yukon Gold potatoes, peeled and cubed
- 1/2 stick butter, softened
- 2 tablespoons spring garlic, minced
- 1/4 cup milk
- 1/3 cup sour cream
- 1/2 teaspoon dried oregano
- 1/2 teaspoon dried rosemary
- 1/2 teaspoon paprika
- Salt and ground black pepper, to taste

Directions

1. Add 1 cup of water and steamer basket to the base of your Instant Pot.

2. Place cubed potatoes in the steamer basket; transfer it to the Instant Pot. Secure the lid. Select the "Manual" mode; cook for 4 minutes under High pressure.

3. Once cooking is complete, use a quick release; carefully remove the lid.

4. Meanwhile, heat a pan over a moderate heat. Melt the butter and cook spring garlic until it is tender and aromatic.

5. Add the milk and scrape up any browned bits with a spatula. Allow it to cool slightly.

6. In a mixing bowl, mash the cooked potatoes. Add the butter/garlic mixture along with the other ingredients.

7. Taste, adjust the seasonings and serve warm. Bon appétit!

BOK CHOY WITH BLACK SESAME

AND OLIVES

Preparation Time: 10 minutes

Servings 4

Nutrition Values: 178 Calories; 10.8g Fat; 14.3g Carbs; 12.8g Protein; 2.1g Sugars

Ingredients

- 1 pound Bok choy, leaves separated
- 2 teaspoons canola oil
- 3 tablespoons black sesame seeds
- 2 tablespoons soy sauce
- 1/2 teaspoon smoked paprika
- Salt and ground black pepper, to taste
- 1/2 cup Kalamata olives, pitted and sliced

Directions

1. Prepare the Instant Pot by adding 1 ½ cups of water and a steamer basket to the bottom. Place the Bok choy in the steamer basket.

2. Secure the lid. Select the "Manual" mode and cook for 4 minutesunder High pressure. Once cooking is complete, use a quick pressure release; carefully remove the lid.

3. Transfer the Bok choy to a bowl and toss with the remaining ingredients. Bon appétit!

RUSSET POTATO BITES

Preparation Time: 15 minutes

Servings 6

Nutrition Values: 221 Calories; 11.2g Fat; 27.9g Carbs; 3.4g Protein; 1g Sugars

Ingredients

- 2 pounds russet potatoes, peeled and diced
- 1/2 stick butter, melted
- 2 garlic cloves, pressed
- 1/2 teaspoon mustard powder
- 1/2 teaspoon sea salt
- 1/4 teaspoon ground black pepper
- 1/2 teaspoon cayenne pepper
- 1 teaspoon thyme
- 2 tablespoons mayonnaise
- 2 tablespoons balsamic vinegar

Directions

1. Add a metal rack and 1 cup of water to your Instant Pot. Place the potatoes on the rack.

2. Secure the lid. Select the "Steam" mode and cook for 10 minutes under High pressure. Once cooking is complete, use a quick pressure release; carefully remove the lid.

3. Cut your potatoes into wedges and toss them with the remaining ingredients. Serve at room temperature. Bon appétit!

STEAMED ROOT VEGGIES WITH SPICY HORSERADISH MAYO

Preparation Time: 10 minutes

Servings 4

Nutrition Values: 116 Calories; 9.7g Fat; 5.2g Carbs; 2.4g Protein; 2.6g Sugars

Ingredients

- 1 1/3 cups water
- 1 celery with leaves, chopped

- 1 turnip, sliced

- 1 carrot, sliced

- 1 red onion, sliced

- 1/4 teaspoon dried dill weed

- 1 teaspoon garlic powder

- 1/2 teaspoon sea salt

- 1/2 teaspoon ground pepper

- 2 tablespoons fresh parsley

For the Horseradish Mayo:

- 1 tablespoon horseradish, well drained

- 1/2 cup mayonnaise

- 2 teaspoons Dijon mustard

Directions

1. Add 1 1/3 cups of water andsteamer basket to the Instant Pot.

2. Arrange celery, turnip, carrot, and onion in the steamer basket. Season the vegetables with dried dill weed, garlic powder, sea salt, and ground pepper.

3. Secure the lid and choose the "Manual" mode, High pressure and 3 minutes. Once cooking is complete, use a quick release; remove the lid carefully.

4. In a mixing bowl, combine the horseradish, mayonnaise, and Dijon mustard. Garnish steamed vegetables with fresh parsley; serve with the horseradish mayo on the side. Bon appétit!

STEAMED BROCCOLI WITH SEEDS

Preparation Time: 10 minutes

Servings 4

Nutrition Values: 199 Calories; 15.6g Fat; 9.9g Carbs; 8.7g Protein; 2.9g Sugars

Ingredients

- 1 head (1 ½-pound) broccoli, broken into florets

- 2 tablespoons extra-virgin olive oil

- 2 garlic cloves, pressed

- 2 tablespoons mayonnaise

- 2 tablespoons balsamic vinegar

- 1 teaspoon Dijon mustard

- Salt and black pepper, to taste

- 1/2 teaspoon dried basil

- 1/2 teaspoon dried oregano

- 1 teaspoon dried parsley flakes

- 2 tablespoons pepitas

- 2 tablespoons sunflower seeds

- 2 tablespoons sesame seeds

Directions

1. Add 1 cup of water and a steamer basket to the bottom of your Instant Pot. Place broccoli florets in the steamer basket.

2. Secure the lid and choose the "Steam" mode; cook for 6 minutes under High pressure. Once cooking is complete, use a quick release; carefully remove the lid.

3. While the broccoli is still hot, add the remaining ingredients. Toss to combine and serve at room temperature.

BUTTERY WAX BEANS WITH SUNFLOWER KERNELS

Preparation Time: 10 minutes

Servings 6

Nutrition Values: 115 Calories; 6.8g Fat; 11.2g Carbs; 4.2g Protein; 3.1g Sugars

Ingredients

- 2 pounds wax beans
- 1 red onion, finely chopped
- 1 teaspoon garlic, smashed
- 1 ½ cups chicken stock
- Black pepper, to taste
- 1/2 teaspoon cayenne pepper
- 2 tablespoons butter, melted
- 1 tablespoon fresh Italian parsley, roughly chopped
- 2 tablespoons toasted sunflower kernels

Directions

1. Add wax beans, onion, garlic, stock, black pepper, cayenne pepper, and butter to the Instant Pot.
2. Secure the lid and choose the "Steam" mode; cook for 3 minutes under High pressure. Once cooking is complete, use a quick release; carefully remove the lid.
3. Transfer cooked beans to a serving bowl; garnish with parsley and sunflower kernels and serve right now. Bon appétit!

BUTTERY BRUSSELS SPROUTS AND CARROTS

Preparation Time: 15 minutes

Servings 4

Nutrition Values: 211 Calories; 14.4g Fat; 17.8g Carbs; 6g Protein; 5.6g Sugars

Ingredients

- 1/2 stick butter, softened
- 1/2 cup shallots, chopped
- 2 cloves garlic, minced
- 1 pound Brussels sprouts
- 4 carrots, chunked
- 1/4 cup lager beer
- 1/4 cup stock, preferably homemade
- 1/4 cup fresh chives, for garnish

Directions

1. Press the "Sauté" button to heat up the Instant Pot. Melt the butter; now, sweat the shallots until tender and fragrant, about 4 minutes.
2. Add garlic and continue to cook for 30 seconds more. Stir in Brussels sprouts, carrots, beer, and stock.
3. Secure the lid and choose the "Manual" setting, High pressure and 8 minutes. Once cooking is complete, use a quick release; carefully remove the lid.
4. Serve garnished with the fresh chives. Enjoy!

MUSTARD CIPOLLINI ONIONS

Preparation Time: 15 minutes

Servings 4

Nutrition Values: 96 Calories; 0.9g Fat; 19.9g Carbs; 3.4g Protein; 12.1g Sugars

Ingredients

- 1 ½ pounds Cipollini onions, outer layer eliminated
- 3/4 cup roasted vegetable stock

- Sea salt and ground black pepper, to taste
- 2 bay leaves
- 1 rosemary sprig
- 1 thyme sprig
- 2 teaspoons honey
- 1 tablespoon mustard
- 1 ½ tablespoons corn starch

Directions

1. Add all ingredients to your Instant Pot. Secure the lid and choose the "Steam" mode. Cook for 10 minutes at High pressure.

2. Once cooking is complete, use a quick release; carefully remove the lid.

3. Arrange the onions on a serving platter and serve warm. Enjoy!

SPICY EGGPLANT WITH STEAMED EGGS

Preparation Time: 50 minutes

Servings 4

Nutrition Values: 235 Calories; 15.8g Fat; 13.5g Carbs; 11.4g Protein; 7.7g Sugars

Ingredients

- 1 pound eggplant, peeled and cut pieces
- 2 teaspoons salt
- 2 tablespoons butter, at room temperature
- 2 garlic cloves, smashed
- 1/2 cup scallions, chopped
- 1 red bell pepper, chopped
- 1 jalapeño pepper, minced
- 2 ripe tomatoes, chopped
- Sea salt, to taste
- 1/2 teaspoon freshly ground black pepper
- 4 eggs

Directions

1. Toss the eggplant with the salt and allow it to sit for 30 minutes; then, drain and rinse the eggplant.

2. Press the "Sauté" button to heat up the Instant Pot. Once hot, melt the butter. Stir in the eggplant and cook for 3 to 5 minutes, stirring periodically.

3. Add the garlic, scallions, peppers, and tomatoes; cook an additional 4 minutes. Season with salt and pepper.

4. Secure the lid. Select the "Manual" setting; cook for 8 minutesat HIGH pressure.Once cooking is complete, use a quick release; carefully remove the lid. Reserve.

5. Add 1 cup of water and metal rack to the Instant Pot. Crack the eggs into ramekins; lower the ramekins onto the rack.

6. Secure the lid. Select the "Steam" setting; cook for 5 minutes under High pressure. Serve with the eggplant mixture on the side. Bon appétit!

COLBY CHEESE AND BEER MASHED CAULIFLOWER

Preparation Time: 20 minutes

Servings 5

Nutrition Values: 297 Calories; 23.6g Fat;

8.9g Carbs; 12.8g Protein; 1.4g Sugars

Ingredients

- 1 1/3 cups water
- 1 cauliflower head
- 1/2 teaspoon cayenne pepper
- Sea salt and freshly ground black pepper
- 2 tablespoons butter
- 1 ½ tablespoons arrowroot powder
- 1/2 cup beer
- 1 teaspoon garlic powder
- 1 ½ cup Colby cheese, shredded
- 1/2 cup sour cream

Directions

1. Add 1 1/3 cups of water to your Instant Pot.

2. Put the cauliflower head into the steaming basket. Transfer the steaming basket to the Instant Pot.

3. Secure the lid and choose the "Manual" button, High pressure and 5 minutes. Once cooking is complete, use a quick release; carefully remove the lid.

4. Season cooked cauliflower with cayenne pepper, salt, and ground black pepper. Mash cooked cauliflower with a potato masher.

5. Next, melt butter in a pan that is preheated over moderate heat. Whisk in the arrowroot powder and cook for 40 seconds, stirring continuously.

6. Gradually pour in beer, stirring continuously. Add the garlic powder and cook until the sauce has thickened, for 3 to 4 minutes.

7. Remove from heat and stir in Colby cheese and sour cream; stir until the cheese has melted. Add mashed cauliflower and stir until everything is well incorporated. Bon appétit!

ZUPPA DI POMODORO

Preparation Time: 30 minutes

Servings 4

Nutrition Values: 175 Calories; 11.1g Fat; 12.5g Carbs; 7.7g Protein; 6.7g Sugars

Ingredients

- 1 tablespoon olive oil
- A bunch of scallions, chopped
- 1 garlic clove, minced
- 2 carrots, grated
- 1 celery, chopped
- 1 pounds tomatoes, seeded and chopped
- 4 cups roasted-vegetable broth
- Sea salt, to taste
- 1/4 teaspoon freshly ground black pepper
- 1/2 teaspoon cayenne pepper
- 1/2 teaspoon dried basil
- 1/2 teaspoon dried oregano
- 1/2 cup double cream
- 1 tablespoon fresh Italian parsley, roughly chopped

Directions

1. Press the "Sauté" button to heat up the Instant Pot. Now, heat the oil; sauté the scallions, garlic, carrot, and celery approximately 5 minutes.

2. Stir in the tomatoes, broth, salt, black pepper, cayenne pepper, basil, and oregano.

3. Secure the lid. Select the "Soup" setting; cook for 20 minutes at High pressure. Once cooking is complete, use a natural pressure release; carefully remove the lid.

4. Fold in the cream and purée the soup with an immersion blender. Serve topped with fresh parsley. Bon appétit!

BROCCOLI WITH TWO-CHEESE AND CHILI DIP

Preparation Time: 15 minutes

Servings 6

Nutrition Values: 246 Calories; 14.5g Fat; 13.6g Carbs; 17.1g Protein; 2.8g Sugars

Ingredients

- 1 cup water
- 1 ½ pounds broccoli, broken into florets

For the Sauce:

- 1 (15-ounces) can of chili
- 1 cup Ricotta cheese, crumbled
- 1 ¼ cups Gruyère cheese shredded
- 1/4 cup salsa

Directions

1. Add water to the base of your Instant Pot.

2. Put the broccoli florets into the steaming basket. Transfer the steaming basket to the Instant Pot.

3. Secure the lid. Choose the "Manual" mode and High pressure; cook for 3

minutes. Once cooking is complete, use a quick pressure release; carefully remove the lid.

4. Now, cook all sauce ingredients in a sauté pan that is preheated over medium-low flame. Cook for 7 minutes or until everything is incorporated.

5. Serve steamed broccoli with the sauce on the side. Bon appétit!

WINTER ROOT VEGETABLE SOUP

Preparation Time: 45 minutes

Servings 8

Nutrition Values: 150 Calories; 6.7g Fat; 18.9g Carbs; 4.7g Protein; 3.3g Sugars

Ingredients

- 2 stalks celery, chopped
- 2 parsnips, chopped
- 2 carrots, chopped
- 1 pound potatoes, cubed
- 1/2 pound turnip, chopped
- 1 onion, chopped
- 2 garlic cloves, minced
- 4 cups water, or as needed
- 3 cups chicken stock
- 1/2 stick butter, at room temperature
- 1/2 teaspoon mustard seeds
- 2 bay leaves
- 1 teaspoon paprika
- 1/2 teaspoon ground black pepper
- Salt, to taste

Directions

1. Place the celery, parsnip, carrots, potatoes, turnip, onion and garlic in the Instant Pot; now, pour in the water and stock.

2. Secure the lid. Select the "Soup" setting; cook for 25 minutes at High pressure. Once cooking is complete, use a quick pressure release; carefully remove the lid.

3. Stir in the butter and seasonings; press the "Sauté" button and continue to cook the soup for 14 to 16 minutes more or until everything is heated through. Discard bay leaves and serve hot.

BROCCOLI AND CELERY CHOWDER

Preparation Time: 35 minutes

Servings 6

Nutrition Values: 193 Calories; 5.5g Fat; 28.6g Carbs; 9.2g Protein; 2.1g Sugars

Ingredients

- 1/2 cup leeks, chopped
- 1 pound broccoli, broken into small florets
- 1/2 pound celery, chopped
- 1 carrot, sliced
- 2 potatoes, peeled and diced
- 3 cups water
- 2 cups roasted-vegetable stock
- Kosher salt, to taste
- 1/4 teaspoon ground black pepper
- 1/4 teaspoon red pepper flakes, crushed
- 1 cup sour cream

Directions

1. Simply place all of the above ingredients, except for sour cream, in your Instant Pot.

2. Secure the lid. Select the "Soup" setting; cook for 30 minutes at High pressure. Once cooking is complete, use a quick pressure release; carefully remove the lid.

3. Then, puree the soup with an immersion blender. Serve in individual bowls, garnished with a dollop of sour cream. Bon appétit!

GOLDEN POTATO AND CAULIFLOWER SOUP

Preparation Time: 35 minutes

Servings 6

Nutrition Values: 175 Calories; 8.2g Fat; 13.9g Carbs; 11.7g Protein; 2.7g Sugars

Ingredients

- 1 pound cauliflower, broken into florets
- 1/2 pound yellow potatoes, diced
- 1 carrot, sliced
- 1 celery, chopped
- 2 garlic cloves, pressed
- 1/2 cup yellow onion, chopped
- 4 cups vegetable broth
- 1 cup water
- 1/2 teaspoon turmeric powder
- 1/4 teaspoon ground black pepper
- 1/2 teaspoon sea salt
- 1/2 teaspoon mustard seeds

- 1 cup yellow Swiss cheese, shredded

Directions

1. Throw all of the above ingredients, except for Swiss cheese, into the Instant Pot.

2. Secure the lid. Select the "Soup" setting; cook for 30 minutes at High pressure. Once cooking is complete, use a quick pressure release; carefully remove the lid.

3. After that, puree the soup with an immersion blender. Divide the soup among six soup bowls; top each serving with shredded Swiss cheese. Bon appétit!

CHINESE-STYLE VEGETABLE SOUP

Preparation Time: 15 minutes

Servings 4

Nutrition Values: 117 Calories; 8.7g Fat; 7.6g Carbs; 3.4g Protein; 4.6g Sugars

Ingredients

- 2 tablespoons sesame oil, softened
- 2 shallots, chopped
- 2 cloves garlic, smashed
- 1/2 pound mushroom, sliced
- 2 carrots, trimmed and chopped
- Sea salt and freshly ground pepper, to taste
- 1/2 teaspoon dried dill
- 1 teaspoon smoked paprika
- 2 tablespoons mijiu (rice wine)
- 3 cups water
- 1/2 cup milk

- 1 tablespoon light soy sauce
- 2 tablespoons fresh parsley, roughly chopped

Directions

1. Press the "Sauté" button and heat the oil. Once hot, sweat the shallots and garlic until tender and translucent.

2. Add mushrooms and carrots. Season with salt, ground pepper, dill, and paprika. Sauté for 3 more minutes more or until the carrots have softened. Add rice wine to deglaze the pan.

3. Add water, milk, and light soy sauce. Secure the lid. Choose the "Manual" function, High pressure and 5 minutes.

4. Once cooking is complete, use a quick release; carefully remove the lid. Taste, adjust the seasonings and serve in individual bowls, garnished with fresh parsley. Bon appétit!

VEGETARIAN MUSHROOM STROGANOFF

Preparation Time: 45 minutes

Servings 8

Nutrition Values: 137 Calories; 3.9g Fat; 23g Carbs; 4.5g Protein; 2.8g Sugars

Ingredients

- 2 tablespoons olive oil
- 1 cup shallots, chopped
- 2 garlic cloves, minced
- 2 russet potatoes, chopped
- 1 celery with leaves, chopped
- 1 bell pepper, seeded and thinly sliced

- 1 habanero pepper, minced
- 14 ounces brown mushrooms, thinly sliced
- 1 cup water
- 1 cup vegetable stock
- Sea salt and ground black pepper, to taste
- 1/2 teaspoon Hungarian paprika
- 1/2 teaspoon cayenne pepper
- 2 bay leaves
- 1 ripe tomato, seeded and chopped
- 2 tablespoons corn flour, plus 3 tablespoons of water

Directions

1. Press the "Sauté" button to heat up the Instant Pot. Then, heat the olive oil and sauté the shallot, garlic, potatoes, and celery until they are softened; add a splash of vegetable stock, if needed.

2. Stir in the mushrooms, water, stock, paprika, cayenne pepper, bay leaves, and tomatoes.

3. Secure the lid. Select the "Meat/Stew" setting; cook for 35 minutes at High pressure. Once cooking is complete, use a quick pressure release; carefully remove the lid.

4. Make the slurry by whisking the corn flour with 3 tablespoons of water. Add the slurry back to the Instant Pot and press the "Sauté" button one more time.

5. Allow it to cook until the liquid has thickened. Discard bay leaves and serve warm.

ACORN SQUASH AND CANDY ONION SOUP

Preparation Time: 25 minutes

Servings 6

Nutrition Values: 365 Calories; 23.3g Fat; 32.1g Carbs; 8.8g Protein; 16.8g Sugars

Ingredients

- 2 tablespoons ghee, melted
- 1 cup candy onions, chopped
- 1 garlic clove, minced
- 2 bell peppers, deveined and chopped
- 1 ½ pounds acorn squash, shredded
- 1 carrot, chopped
- 1 celery, chopped
- 6 ounces cream cheese
- 1 bay leaf
- 2 cups water
- 4 cups vegetable stock

Directions

1. Press the "Sauté" button to heat up the Instant Pot; melt the ghee and sauté candy onions, garlic and peppers until they are softened.

2. Add the remaining ingredients.

3. Secure the lid. Select the "Soup" setting; cook for 20 minutes at High pressure. Once cooking is complete, use a quick pressure release; carefully remove the lid.

4. Afterwards, purée the soup with an immersion blender and serve hot. Enjoy!

AROMATIC SNOW PEAS

Preparation Time: 10 minutes

Servings 4

Nutrition Values: 126 Calories; 5.4g Fat; 16.9g Carbs; 3.6g Protein; 8.1g Sugars

Ingredients

- 1 ½ tablespoons coconut oil

- 1 pound snow peas,frozen

- 2 carrots, sliced

- 1 parsnip, sliced

- Seasoned salt, to taste

- 1 cup water

- 1/2 teaspoon ground black pepper

- 1/2 teaspoon red pepper flakes, crushed

- 1 tablespoon white sugar

Directions

1. Add all of the above ingredients to your Instant Pot.

2. Secure the lid. Select the "Steam" setting; cook for 4 minutes at High pressure. Once cooking is complete, use a quick pressure release; carefully remove the lid.

3. Transfer everything to a serving dish. Enjoy!

VEGETABLES

DELICIOUS INSTANT POT RATATOUILLE

Servings: 4

Preparation time: 10 minutes

Cooking Time: 20 minutes

Ingredients:

- 14 ounces squash, chopped
- 4 tomatoes, chopped
- 14 ounces eggplant, chopped
- Salt and black pepper to the taste
- 1 red capsicum, chopped
- 1 green capsicum, chopped
- 2 yellow onions, chopped
- 1 tablespoon extra virgin olive oil
- 3 garlic cloves, finely minced
- ½ teaspoon thyme, dried
- 2 teaspoons basil, dried

Directions:

1. Heat up your instant pot with the oil, add garlic and onion, stir and cook for 4 minutes.
2. Add squash, eggplant, red and green capsicum, tomatoes, thyme, salt, pepper and basil, stir, cover and cook on High for 10 minutes.
3. Release pressure naturally for 5 minutes, divide amongst plates and serve right away.
4. Enjoy!

Nutrition Values: Calories 154, fat 10, carbs 10, fiber 3.2, sugar 5, protein 1.7

INSTANT POT POTATO SALAD

Servings: 6

Preparation time: 10 minutes

Cooking Time: 10 minutes

Ingredients:

- 1 small yellow onion, chopped
- 6 red potatoes
- 1 celery stalk, chopped
- 1 cup water
- Salt and black pepper to the taste
- 3 teaspoons dill, finely chopped
- 1 teaspoon mustard
- 1 teaspoon cider vinegar
- 3 ounces vegan mayonnaise

Directions:

1. Put potatoes in your instant pot, add the water, cover and cook on High for 3 minutes.
2. Release pressure for another 3 minutes, leave potatoes to cool down, peel, chop them and put them in a salad bowl.
3. Add chopped onion, celery, salt, pepper and the dill and stir everything.
4. In a bowl, mix vegan mayo with vinegar and mustard and stir well.
5. Add this to the salad, toss to coat and

serve.

6. Enjoy!

Nutrition Values: Calories 140, fat 2, carbs 24, fiber 2, sugar 2, protein 4

TASTY INSTANT POT VEGGIE DISH

Servings: 4

Preparation time: 10 minutes

Cooking Time: 10 minutes

Ingredients:

- ½ cup canola oil
- ¾ cup red lentils, soaked overnight and drained
- 1 yellow onion, finely chopped
- 1 garlic clove, minced
- ¼ cup parsley, chopped
- ¼ cup dill, chopped
- 1 teaspoon basil, finely chopped
- 3 tomatoes, chopped
- 1 cup veggie stock
- 4 potatoes, chopped
- 2 zucchinis, chopped
- 2 cups peas, frozen
- 3 celery stalks, chopped
- 2 carrots, chopped
- 1 green bell pepper, thinly sliced
- Salt and black pepper to the taste

Directions:

1. Heat up a pan with the oil over medium high heat, add onion, stir and cook for 2 minutes.

2. Add parsley, garlic and dill, stir, cook

1 minute and transfer everything to your instant pot.

3. Add lentils, stock, basil, tomatoes, zucchinis, potatoes, carrots, green bell pepper, celery, peas, salt and pepper to the taste, stir, cover and cook on High for 6 minutes.

4. Release pressure naturally for 10 minutes, add more salt and pepper to the taste, divide amongst plates and serve.

5. Enjoy!

Nutrition Values: Calories 240, fat 5, carbs 12, fiber 6, protein 30

CARROTS CASSEROLE

Servings: 4

Preparation time: 10 minutes

Cooking Time: 10 minutes

Ingredients:

- 3 tablespoons vegetable oil
- 1 teaspoon lemon juice
- ¼ cup breadcrumbs
- 1 and ¾ cup water
- 1 tablespoon parsley, finely chopped
- 1 pound carrots, cut into thin matchsticks
- 1 pound broccoli
- Salt and black pepper to the taste

Directions:

1. Heat up a pan with the oil over medium high heat, add breadcrumbs, stir and cook until they become golden.

2. Transfer them to a bowl, add parsley

and lemon juice, stir well and leave aside for now.

3. In your instant pot, mix carrots with broccoli, salt and pepper to the taste, add the water, cover and cook on High for 10 minutes.

4. Release pressure naturally, drain veggie and divide them amongst plates.

5. Sprinkle bread crumbs mix all over them and serve right away.

6. Enjoy!

Nutrition Values: Calories 170, fat 5, carbs 13, fiber 5.6, protein 20

SPECIAL INSTANT POT PEAS AND POTATOES DISH

Servings: 6

Preparation time: 10 minutes

Cooking Time: 10 minutes

Ingredients:

- 1 cup peas, frozen
- 6 potatoes, chopped
- 1 teaspoon cumin seeds
- 1 yellow onion, chopped
- 2 green chili peppers, chopped
- 2 tablespoons canola oil
- 2 tomatoes, finely diced
- 1 teaspoon ginger paste
- 1 teaspoon garlic paste
- 1 teaspoon cumin powder
- 2 teaspoons coriander powder
- 1 teaspoon mango powder
- ½ teaspoon turmeric powder

- 1 teaspoon red chili powder
- 1 teaspoon garam masala
- Salt to the taste
- ½ cup water
- 2 tablespoons coriander, finely chopped

Directions:

1. Heat up a pan with the oil over medium high heat, add cumin seeds and toast them for 1 minute.

2. Add chili peppers, stir and cook for 3 minutes.

3. Add onions, stir and cook for 2 minutes more.

4. Add ginger and garlic paste, stir, cook for 1 minute more and transfer to your instant pot.

5. Add tomatoes, potatoes, peas, coriander, cumin powder, red chili powder, turmeric powder, mango powder, salt to the taste and water.

6. Stir, cover pot and cook on High for 7 minutes.

7. Release pressure naturally, add garam masala and coriander, stir, divide amongst plates and serve.

8. Enjoy!

Nutrition Values: Calories 163, fat 5, carbs 24, fiber 2, sugar 1, protein 3

INSTANT POT RED CABBAGE SALAD

Servings: 4

Preparation time: 5 minutes

Cooking Time: 5 minutes

Ingredients:

- 2 cups red cabbage, shredded
- 1 tablespoon canola oil
- Salt and black pepper to the taste
- ¼ cup white onion, finely chopped
- 2 teaspoons red wine vinegar
- ½ teaspoon palm sugar

Directions:

1. Put shredded cabbage in your instant pot, add some water, cover and cook on High for 5 minutes.
2. Release pressure naturally, drain water and transfer it to a salad bowl.
3. Add salt, pepper to the taste, onion, oil, palm sugar and vinegar, toss to coat and serve right away.
4. Enjoy!

Nutrition Values: Calories 110, fat 1, carbs 6, fiber 2.2, sugar 2, protein 1.1

INSTANT POT VEGAN CABBAGE ROLLS

Servings: 6

Preparation time: 15 minutes

Cooking Time: 35 minutes

Ingredients:

- 1 tablespoon extra virgin olive oil
- 1 cup brown rice, uncooked
- 9 and ½ cups water
- 3 cups mushrooms, chopped
- 1 yellow onion, chopped
- 2 garlic cloves, minced
- Salt and black pepper to the taste
- 12 green cabbage leaves
- ½ teaspoon walnuts, finely chopped
- ½ teaspoon caraway seeds
- A pinch of cayenne pepper
- Tomato sauce for serving

Directions:

1. Put 1 and ½ cups water and the rice in your instant pot, cover and cook on High for 15 minutes.
2. Release pressure automatically, rinse rice under cold water, drain it well and put it in a bowl.
3. Heat up a pan with the oil over medium high heat, add onion, mushrooms and garlic, stir and cook for 5 minutes.
4. Add caraway, walnuts, salt, pepper, and cayenne, pour over rice and stir very well.
5. Pour 8 cups water in a pot, bring to a boil over medium high heat, add cabbage leaves, cook for 1 minute, drain and rinse them under cold water.
6. Arrange them on a working surface, place 1/3 cup rice mix in the middle of each, roll them, seal edges and place them in your instant pot.
7. Add 1-inch water, cover and cook on High pressure for 10 minutes.
8. Release pressure, divide them between plates and serve them with some tomato sauce on top.
9. Enjoy!

Nutrition Values: Calories 283, fat 10, carbs 30, fiber 6, protein 5, sugar 3

SIMPLE INSTANT POT TOMATO

AND GREEN BEANS STEW

Servings: 4

Preparation time: 10 minutes

Cooking Time: 10 minutes

Ingredients:

- 1 tablespoon extra virgin olive oil
- 1 garlic clove, crushed
- 14 ounces canned tomatoes, chopped
- 1 pound green beans
- Salt to the taste
- 1 sprigs basil, leaves chopped

Directions:

1. Heat up a pan with the oil over medium high heat, add garlic, stir, cook for 2 minutes and transfer to your instant pot.
2. Add tomatoes, green beans and salt to the taste, cover pot and cook on High for 5 minutes.
3. Release pressure naturally, transfer to a bowl, add more salt if needed, sprinkle basil and serve.
4. Enjoy!

Nutrition Values: Calories 60, fat 3.2, carbs 1.4, fiber 2.6, protein 1.5

SPECIAL TOMATO AND ZUCCHINI DISH

Servings: 3

Preparation time: 10 minutes

Cooking Time: 10 minutes

Ingredients:

- 1 tablespoon vegetable oil

- 1 pound colored cherry tomatoes
- 2 yellow onions, chopped
- 1 cup tomato puree
- Salt and black pepper to the taste
- 2 garlic cloves, minced
- 6 zucchinis, chopped
- A drizzle of olive oil
- 1 bunch basil, finely chopped

Directions:

1. Heat up a pan with the vegetable oil over medium high heat, add onions, stir and sauté those for 5 minutes.
2. Transfer this to your instant pot, add zucchini, tomatoes, salt, pepper, and tomato puree, cover and cook on High for 5 minutes.
3. Release pressure naturally, add garlic and basil, more salt and pepper if needed and a drizzle of olive oil.
4. Toss to coat, divide amongst plates and serve.
5. Enjoy!

Nutrition Values: Calories 70, fat 1, carbs 6, fiber 2.8, sugar 4, protein 2

SUMMER VEGETABLE MIX

Servings: 4

Preparation time: 10 minutes

Cooking Time: 10 minutes

Ingredients:

- 1 eggplant, cut into medium chunks
- ¼ cup extra virgin olive oil
- 1 yellow bell pepper, cut into thin strips

- 2 zucchinis, cut into small pieces

- Salt and black pepper to the taste

- 2 potatoes, chopped

- 1 yellow onion, cut into wedges

- 10 cherry tomatoes, cut in halves

- 2 tablespoons pine nuts

- 1 tablespoon capers, drained

- 1 tablespoon raisins

- 1 cup water

- ¼ cup olives, pitted and roughly chopped

- 1 bunch basil leaves, chopped

Directions:

1. Put eggplant pieces in a strainer, sprinkle salt, leave them aside for a few minutes, press them to get rid of the liquid and transfer them to your instant pot.

2. Add olive oil, potatoes, onion, zucchinis, bell pepper, tomatoes, capers, pine nuts, raisins, olives, half of the basil and the water, cover pot and cook on High for 7 minutes.

3. Release pressure, add salt and pepper to the taste, the rest of the basil, stir gently, divide amongst plates and serve.

4. Enjoy!

Nutrition Values: Calories 131, fat 7.3, carbs 16, fiber 4.7, sugar 7, protein 3.5

APPLE ALMOND RICE MEAL

Preparation Time: 8-10min.

Cooking Time: 35 min.

Servings: 6

Ingredients:

- 1 chopped pear
- 3 ½ cups water
- 1 ½ cups wild rice
- 1 cup dried, mixed fruit
- 2 small apples, peeled and chopped
- ½ cup almonds, slivered
- 2 tablespoons apple juice
- 1 teaspoon cinnamon
- 1 tablespoon maple syrup
- 1 teaspoon veggie oil
- ½ teaspoon ground nutmeg
- Pepper and salt as needed

Directions:

1. Take Instant Pot and carefully arrange it over a clean, dry kitchen platform. Turn on the appliance.

2. In the cooking pot area, add the rice and water. Stir the ingredients gently.

3. Close the pot lid and seal the valve to avoid any leakage. Find and press "Manual" cooking setting and set cooking time to 30 minutes.

4. Allow the recipe ingredients to cook for the set time, and after that, the timer reads "zero".

5. Meanwhile, soak the dried fruit in just enough apple juice to cover everything in a bowl. Set aside for 30 minutes and then drain the fruit.

6. Press "Cancel" and press "NPR" setting for natural pressure release. It takes 8-10 times for all inside pressure to release.

7. Open the pot and transfer the mixture to serving bowl.

8. Find and press "Sauté" cooking function.

9. In the cooking pot area; add the oil, apples, pears, and almonds in the pot. Cook for 2 minutes to cook well and soften.

10. Mix in 2 tablespoon apple juice and keep cooking for a few minutes more. Mix in the syrup, cooked rice, soaked fruit, and seasonings.

11. Cook for 2-3 minutes and serve warm!

Nutrition Values:

CALORIES: 224

Fat: 3g

Carbohydrates: 38g

Fiber: 5.5g

Protein: 6.5g

MULTIGRAIN RISOTTO

Preparation Time: 5min.

Cooking Time: 20-22 min.

Servings: 6

Ingredients:

- 1 cup mixture of quinoa, millet, bulgur, oats, and buckwheat, or any other grains of your choice, soaked in water overnight, drained
- 1 cup coconut milk
- 4 cups water
- Sweetener as needed (optional)

Directions:

1. **Take Instant Pot and carefully arrange it over a clean, dry kitchen platform. Turn on the appliance.**

2. **In the cooking pot area, add the mentioned ingredients. Stir the ingredients gently.**

3. **Close the pot lid and seal the valve to avoid any leakage. Find and press "Porridge" cooking setting with default cooking time.**

4. **Allow the recipe ingredients to cook for the set time, and after that, the timer reads "zero".**

5. **Press "Cancel" and press "NPR" setting for natural pressure release. It takes 8-10 times for all inside pressure to release.**

6. **Open the pot and arrange the cooked recipe in serving plates. Enjoy the vegan recipe!**

Nutrition Values:

Calories: 191

Fat: 10.5g

Carbohydrates: 22.5g

Fiber: 3g

Protein: 4.5g

GARLIC BEAN RICE MEAL

Preparation Time: 10 min.

Cooking Time: 25 min.

Servings: 4

Ingredients:

- 2 tablespoons olive oil
- 2 cloves garlic, minced
- 1 cup brown rice, rinsed
- 1 cup black beans, rinsed
- 1 medium onion, chopped
- 4 ½ cups water
- ½ avocado, sliced to serve
- Salt as needed
- 2 teaspoons lime juice

Directions:

1. Take Instant Pot and carefully arrange it over a clean, dry kitchen platform. Turn on the appliance.

2. In the cooking pot area, add the mentioned ingredients except for lime juice and avocado. Stir the ingredients gently.

3. Close the pot lid and seal the valve to avoid any leakage. Find and press "Manual" cooking setting and set cooking time to 25 minutes.

4. Allow the recipe ingredients to cook for the set time, and after that, the timer reads "zero".

5. Press "Cancel" and press "NPR" setting for natural pressure release. It takes 8-10 times for all inside pressure to release.

6. Open the pot, fluff the mixture. Add lime juice and stir.

7. Spoon into bowls. Garnish with avocado slices and serve.

Nutrition Values:

Calories: 461

Fat: 14g

Carbohydrates: 66.5g

Fiber: 11g

Protein: 14g

AVOCADO RICE SALAD

Preparation Time: 10min.

Cooking Time: 24 min.

Servings: 6-8

Ingredients:

- 1 can (14 oz.) black beans, drained
- 1 ½ cups water
- ¼ cup cilantro, minced
- 1 cup brown rice
- 1 avocado, diced
- 12 grape tomatoes, make quarters
- ¼ teaspoon salt
- For the dressing:
- 2 teaspoons Tabasco (optional)
- 2 garlic cloves, minced
- 3 tablespoons lime juice
- 3 tablespoons extra-virgin olive oil
- 1/ 8 teaspoon salt
- 1 teaspoon maple syrup

Directions:

1. Take Instant Pot and carefully arrange it over a clean, dry kitchen platform. Turn on the appliance.

2. In the cooking pot area, add the rice and water. Stir the ingredients gently.

3. Close the pot lid and seal the valve to avoid any leakage. Find and press "Manual" cooking setting and set cooking time to 24 minutes.

4. Allow the recipe ingredients to cook for the set time, and after that, the timer reads "zero".

5. Press "Cancel" and press "NPR" setting for natural pressure release. It takes 8-10 times for all inside pressure to release.

6. Open the pot and transfer the mixture to the serving container.

7. Mix the black beans, avocado, tomato, and cilantro.

8. In another mixing bowl, whisk the dressing ingredients together. Pour the dressing over the rice mix and combine; serve!

Nutrition Values:

Calories: 376

Fat: 11g

Carbohydrates: 48g

Fiber: 12g

Protein: 14.5g

SPINACH CHICKPEA RICE MEAL

Preparation Time: 8-10min.

Cooking Time: 25 min.

Servings: 4

Ingredients:

- 1 teaspoon lime juice
- 2 small tomatoes, diced one

- Half inch piece ginger, grated
- ½ teaspoon salt
- 1 tablespoon curry powder
- 1 cup baby spinach
- ½ cup chopped yellow onion
- 2 cups water
- ¼ cup brown rice, cooked
- 1 teaspoon vegetable oil
- 4 garlic cloves, minced
- 1 small acorn squash
- 1 can chickpeas

Directions:

1. Slice squash in half and scrape seeds.
2. Take Instant Pot and carefully arrange it over a clean, dry kitchen platform. Turn on the appliance.
3. Find and press "Sauté" cooking function.
4. In the cooking pot area; add the oil and onions in the pot. Cook for 2-3 minutes to cook well and soften.
5. Add the garlic and cook 1 minute. Mix other ingredients besides squash and cook until spinach is wilted.
6. Place mixture inside each squash half.
7. Pour the water into the cooking pot area. Arrange the trivet inside it; arrange the squash halves over the trivet.
8. Close the pot lid and seal the valve to avoid any leakage. Find and press "Manual" cooking setting and set cooking time to 20 minutes.
9. Allow the recipe ingredients to cook for the set time, and after that, the timer reads "zero".
10. Press "Cancel" and press "NPR" setting for natural pressure release. It takes 8-10 times for all inside pressure to release.
11. Open the pot and arrange the cooked recipe in serving plates. Enjoy the vegan recipe!

Nutrition Values:

Calories –178

Fat: 5g

Carbohydrates: 29.5g

Fiber: 5.5g

Protein: 6g

SORGHUM PUMPKIN MEAL

Preparation Time: 5-8min.

Cooking Time: 25 min.

Servings: 5-6

Ingredients:

- 1½ tablespoons pumpkin pie spice
- 1½ cups almond milk, unsweetened
- 1 ½ teaspoons vanilla extract
- 3 tablespoons maple syrup
- 1 ½ cups sorghum, rinsed
- 1 ¼ cups pumpkin puree
- 3 cups water

Directions:

1. Take Instant Pot and carefully arrange it over a clean, dry kitchen platform. Turn on the appliance.
2. In the cooking pot area, add the mentioned ingredients. Stir the ingredients gently.

3. Close the pot lid and seal the valve to avoid any leakage. Find and press "Manual" cooking setting and set cooking time to 25 minutes.

4. Allow the recipe ingredients to cook for the set time, and after that, the timer reads "zero".

5. Press "Cancel" and press "NPR" setting for natural pressure release. It takes 8-10 times for all inside pressure to release.

6. Open the pot and arrange the cooked recipe in serving plates. Serve with almond milk.

Nutrition Values:

Calories: 227

Fat: 2.5g

Carbohydrates: 49.5g

Fiber: 4.5g

Protein: 7g

SPINACH MUSHROOM RISOTTO

Preparation Time: 5min.

Cooking Time: 8 min.

Servings: 5

Ingredients:

- ½ cup white onion, minced
- 4-ounce mushrooms, chopped
- 1 cup Arborio rice
- 1 ½ tablespoon nutritional yeast
- 3 cups vegetable broth
- 2 cups spinach
- ¼ cup lemon juice
- ½ cup dry white wine
- 1 teaspoon salt
- 1 tablespoon vegan butter
- 1 tablespoon olive oil, optional
- 1 teaspoon thyme
- 3 cloves garlic, minced
- Black pepper as needed

Directions:

1. Take Instant Pot and carefully arrange it over a clean, dry kitchen platform. Turn on the appliance.

2. Find and press "Sauté" cooking function.

3. In the cooking pot area; add the oil, garlic, and onions in the pot. Cook for 2 minutes to cook well and soften.

4. Add the rice and stir well. Pour the broth, mushrooms, wine, thyme, and salt.

5. Close the pot lid and seal the valve to avoid any leakage. Find and press "Manual" cooking setting and set cooking time to 5 minutes.

6. Allow the recipe ingredients to cook for the set time, and after that, the timer reads "zero".

7. Press "Cancel" and press "NPR" setting for natural pressure release. It takes 8-10 times for all inside pressure to release.

8. Open the pot and arrange the cooked recipe in serving plates.

9. Mix the yeast, spinach, vegan butter, and pepper. Stir well and serve warm!

Nutrition Values:

Calories: 323

Fat: 8.5g

Carbohydrates: 43.5g

Fiber: 3.5g

Protein: 10g

GREEN TEA RICE RISOTTO

Preparation Time: 5min.

Cooking Time: 30 min.

Servings: 5-6

Ingredients:

- 1 cup brown rice, rinsed
- ¼ cup lentils, rinsed
- 7 cups water
- 3 green tea bags
- Salt as needed

Directions:

1. Take Instant Pot and carefully arrange it over a clean, dry kitchen platform. Turn on the appliance.

2. In the cooking pot area, add the mentioned ingredients. Stir the ingredients gently.

3. Close the pot lid and seal the valve to avoid any leakage. Find and press "Manual" cooking setting and set cooking time to 30 minutes.

4. Allow the recipe ingredients to cook for the set time, and after that, the timer reads "zero".

5. Press "Cancel" and press "NPR" setting for natural pressure release. It takes 8-10 times for all inside pressure to release.

6. Open the pot, remove tea bags and arrange the cooked recipe in serving plates. Enjoy the vegan recipe!

Nutrition Values:

Calories: 123

Fat: 1g

Carbohydrates: 24.5g

Fiber: 1.5g

Protein: 3g

MAC WITH ARTICHOKES

Preparation Time: 10 minutes

Cooking Time: 4 minutes

Servings: 4

Ingredients:

- 3 cups vegetable broth
- 1 ½ cup macaroni
- ½ cup artichoke hearts, canned, chopped
- 5 oz vegan Parmesan, grated
- ½ cup spinach, chopped
- ½ teaspoon ground black pepper
- ½ teaspoon chili flakes

Directions:

1. In the instant pot combine together vegetable broth, macaroni, and ground black pepper.

2. Close and seal the lid. Set manual mode (High pressure) and cook macaroni for 4 minutes.

3. Use quick pressure release and open the lid.

4. Add grated cheese, chili flakes, artichokes, and spinach.

5. Mix up the meal till the cheese is melted.

6. The meal is cooked.

Nutrition Values: Calories 263, fat 1.6, fiber 2, carbs 33.4, protein 22.9

PESTO PASTA

Preparation Time: 10 minutes

Cooking Time: 4 minutes

Servings: 5

Ingredients:

- 2 cups fresh basil
- 1 teaspoon minced garlic
- 4 oz pine nuts
- 6 oz vegan Parmesan, grated
- 1/3 cup olive oil
- ½ teaspoon kosher salt
- 12 oz pasta
- 3 cups vegetable broth

Directions:

1. Pour vegetable broth in the instant pot bowl.
2. Add pasta and close the lid.
3. Seal it and cook on High pressure for 4 minutes. Use quick pressure release.
4. Meanwhile, in the food processor blend together grated cheese, pine nuts, minced garlic, basil, kosher salt, and olive oil. When the mixture is smooth: pesto sauce is cooked.
5. Transfer cooked pasta in the serving bowls, add pesto sauce and mix it up carefully before serving.

Nutrition Values: Calories 594, fat 31.4, fiber 1, carbs 48.1, protein 27.9

RICE AND CHICKEN

Preparation Time: 50 minutes

Servings: 2

Ingredients:

- 3 chicken quarters cut into small pieces
- 2 carrots, cut into chunks
- 1 yellow onion, sliced
- 1 tsp. cumin, ground
- 1 tbsp. soy sauce
- 1 tbsp. peanut oil
- 2 potatoes, cut into quarters
- 1 shallot, sliced
- 1 ½ tbsp. cornstarch mixed with 2 tbsp. water
- 1 ½ tsp. turmeric powder
- 1 green bell pepper; chopped
- 7 oz. coconut milk
- 2 bay leaves
- 3 garlic cloves; minced.
- Salt and black pepper to the taste
- For the marinade:
- 1 ½ cups water
- 1 ½ cups rice
- 1 tbsp. white wine
- 1 tbsp. soy sauce
- 1/2 tsp. sugar
- A pinch of white pepper

Directions:

1. In a bowl, mix chicken with sugar, white pepper, 1 tablespoon soy sauce and 1 tablespoon white wine, stir and

keep in the fridge for 20 minutes.

2. Set your instant pot on Sauté mode; add peanut oil and heat it up

3. Add onion and shallot, stir and cook for 3 minutes

4. Add garlic, salt, and pepper, stir and cook for 2 minutes more.

5. Add chicken, stir and brown for 2 minutes

6. Add turmeric and cumin, stir and cook for 1 minute.

7. Add bay leaves, carrots, potatoes, bell pepper, coconut milk and 1 tablespoon soy sauce

8. Stir everything, place steamer basket in the pot, place the rice in a bowl and the basket

9. Add 1 ½ cups water in the bowl, seal the instant pot lid and cook at High for 4 minutes.

10. Release the pressure naturally, take the rice out of the pot and divide among plates, add cornstarch to pot and stir

11. Add chicken next to rice and serve.

TASTY GREEN RICE.

Preparation Time: 50 minutes

Servings: 6

Ingredients:

- 2 cups.rice basmati.
- 1 cup.dill
- 3 oz. butter
- 1 tbsp. salt
- 4 cups.beef broth
- 1 cup.spinach
- 1 tsp. olive oil
- 1 tsp. dried oregano
- 1 tbsp. minced garlic

Directions:

1. Pour the olive oil in the Instant Pot. Add rice, butter, and minced garlic

2. "Sauté" the mixture for 5 minutes. Stir it frequently

3. After this, add beef broth.

4. Wash the spinach and dill carefully. Chop the greens

5. Transfer the chopped greens in the blender and blend them well

6. Then add the blended greens in the rice mixture

7. Add butter, salt, and dried oregano

8. Mix up the mixture carefully with the help of the wooden spoon. After this, close the lid and set the Instant Pot mode RICE

9. Cook the dish for 20 minutes.

10. When the time is over: release the remaining pressure and transfer the green rice in the serving bowl.

SALMON AND RICE

Preparation Time: 10 minutes

Servings: 2

Ingredients:

- 2 wild salmon fillets, frozen
- 1/2 cup jasmine rice
- 1/4 cup vegetable soup mix; dried
- 1 cup chicken stock
- 1 tbsp. butter

- A pinch of saffron
- Salt and black pepper to the taste

Directions:

1. In your instant pot, mix stock with rice, soup mix, butter and saffron and stir.

2. Season salmon with salt and pepper, place in the steamer basket of your pot, close the lid and cook on High for 5 minutes.

3. Quick release the pressure, divide salmon among plates, add rice mix on the side and serve.

STEAMED EGGS WITH RICE

Preparation Time: 15 minutes

Servings: 2

Ingredients:

- 2 eggs
- 1 ⅓ cup water
- 2 scallions; finely chopped
- Salt and black pepper to the taste
- A pinch of sesame seeds
- A pinch of garlic powder
- Hot rice for serving

Directions:

1. In a bowl, mix the eggs with 1/3 cup water and whisk well.

2. Strain this into a heat proof dish

3. Add salt, pepper to the taste, sesame seeds, garlic powder and scallions and whisk very well.

4. Put 1 cup water in your instant pot, place the dish in the steamer basket,

seal the instant pot lid and cook at High for 5 minutes

5. Quick release the pressure, open the instant pot lid, divide the rice among plates and add eggs mix on the side.

MIX RICE MEDLEY.

Preparation Time: 35 minutes

Servings: 4

Ingredients:

- 3/8 to 1/2 tsp. sea salt, optional
- 3/4 cup. (or more) short grain brown rice.
- 2 to 4 tbsp. red, wild or black rice
- 1 tbsp. water
- 1 ½ cups.water

Directions:

1. Put as much as 2 to 4 tablespoons of red, wild, or black rice or use all three kinds in 1-cup measuring cup.

2. Add brown rice to make 1 cup. total of rice. Put the rice in a strainer and wash. Put the rice in the Instant Pot

3. Add 1 ½ cup. plus 1 tablespoon water in the pot. If desired, add salt.

4. Stir and then check the sides of the pot to make sure the rice is pushed down into the water. Close and lock the lid. Press MULTIGRAIN and set the time to 23 minutes.

5. When the timer beeps, let the pressure release naturally for 5 minutes, then turn the steam valve and release the pressure slowly

6. If you have time, let the pressure release naturally for 15 minutes. Stir and serve.

MEXICAN BROWN RICE CASSEROLE.

Preparation Time: 35 minutes

Servings: 4

Ingredients:

- 2 cups.uncooked brown rice
- 5 cups.water
- 1 cup.soaked black beans
- 6 oz. tomato paste
- 2 tsp. chili powder
- 2 tsp. onion powder
- 1 tsp. garlic
- 1 tsp. salt

Directions:

1. A few hours before dinner, put your dry beans in a bowl with enough water to cover them.
2. Soak on the countertop for at least two hours and drain.
3. Put everything in your Instant Pot. Close and seal the pressure cooker. Select "Manual" and then cook on "High" pressure for 28 minutes.
4. When time is up, hit "Cancel" and quick-release
5. Taste and season more if necessary

MEXICAN BASMATI RICE.

Preparation Time: 30 minutes

Servings: 6

Ingredients:

- 2 cups.rice, long-grain, such as Lundberg Farms Brown Basmati.

- 1/2 cup.tomato paste
- 2 tsp. salt
- 1/2 white onion; chopped.
- 3 cloves garlic; minced
- 1 small jalapeño, optional
- 2 cups.water

Directions:

1. Set the Instant Pot to normal "Sauté". Heat the olive oil.
2. Add the garlic, onion, rice, and salt. Sauté for about 3: 4 minutes or until fragrant.
3. Mix the tomato paste with the water until well combined. Pour into the pot. Add the whole jalapeno pepper.
4. Press "Cancel". Close and lock the lid. Press "Pressure", set to "High", and the timer for 3 minutes is using white rice or for 22 minutes if using brown rice.
5. When the timer beeps, release the pressure naturally for about 15 minutes. Turn the steam valve to "Venting". Carefully open the lid
6. Using a fork, fluff the rice and serve hot

DELICIOUS RICE PUDDING

Preparation Time: 45 minutes

Servings: 4

Ingredients:

- 2 cups black rice, washed and rinsed
- 6 ½ cups water
- 3/4 cup sugar
- 5 cardamom pods, crushed.

- 3 cloves
- 1/2 cup coconut, grated
- Chopped mango for serving
- 2 cinnamon sticks
- A pinch of salt

Directions:

1. Put the rice in your instant pot, add a pinch of salt and the water and stir

2. In a cheesecloth bag, mix cardamom with cinnamon and cloves and tie it.

3. Place this in the pot with the rice, close the lid and cook on Low for 35 minutes

4. Release the pressure naturally, open the instant pot lid, stir the rice, add coconut and set your pot to sauté mode

5. Cook for 10 minutes, discard spices bag, transfer to breakfast bowls and serve with chopped mango on top.

WILD RICE &FARRO PILAF

Preparation Time: 45 minutes

Servings: 12

Ingredients:

- 1 ½ cups whole grain faro
- 1 tbsp. parsley and sage; finely chopped
- 1/2 cup hazelnuts, toasted and chopped.
- 3/4 cup wild rice
- 1 shallot; finely chopped
- 1 tsp. garlic; minced.
- 6 cups chicken stock

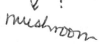

- 3/4 cup cherries; dried
- Some chopped chives for serving
- A drizzle of extra virgin olive oil
- Salt and black pepper to the taste

Directions:

1. Set your instant pot on Sauté mode; add a drizzle of oil and heat it up.

2. Add onion and garlic, stir and cook for 2: 3 minutes.

3. Add farro, rice, salt, pepper, stock and 1 tablespoon mixed sage and parsley; then stir well. seal the instant pot lid and cook on High for 25 minutes.

4. Meanwhile, put cherries in a pot, add hot water to cover, leave aside for 10 minutes and drain them

5. Release the pressure naturally for 5 minutes, then release remaining pressure by turning the valve to 'Venting', now open the instant pot lid, drain excess liquid, add hazelnuts and cherries, stir gently, divide among plates and garnish with chopped chives

GRAIN RICE MILLET BLEND.

Preparation Time: 15 minutes

Servings: 8

Ingredients:

- 2 cups.jasmine rice OR long-grain white rice
- 1/2 tsp. sea salt (optional)
- 3 ¼ cups.water
- 1/2 cup.millet

Directions:

1. Put all the ingredients in the Instant Pot and stir

2. Cover and lock the lid.

3. Press the RICE button and let the pot do all the cooking, about 10 minutes

MEXICAN RICE

Preparation Time: 15 minutes

Servings: 8

Ingredients:

- 1 cup long grain rice
- 1/2 cup cilantro; chopped
- 1/2 avocado, pitted; peeled and chopped.
- 1/4 cup green hot sauce
- 1 ¼ cups veggie stock
- Salt and black pepper to the taste

Directions:

1. Put the rice in your instant pot, add stock; then stir well. close the lid and cook at High for 4 minutes

2. Release the pressure naturally for 10 minutes, then release remaining pressure by turning the valve to 'Venting', open the instant pot lid, fluff it with a fork and transfer to a bowl

3. Meanwhile, in your food processor, mix avocado with hot sauce and cilantro and blend well.

4. Pour this over rice, stir well, add salt and pepper to the taste, stir again, divide among plates and serve

RICE BOWL

Preparation Time: 12 minutes

Servings: 4

Ingredients:

- 1 cup brown rice
- 1 cup coconut milk
- 2 cups water
- 1/2 cup maple syrup
- 1/2 cup coconut chips
- 1/4 cup raisins
- 1/4 cup almonds
- A pinch of cinnamon powder
- A pinch of salt

Directions:

1. Put the rice in a pot, add the water, place on stove over medium high heat, cook according to instructions, drain and transfer it to your instant pot.

2. Add milk, coconut chips, almonds, raisins, salt, cinnamon and maple syrup, stir well, seal the instant pot lid and cook at High for 5 minutes

3. Quick release the pressure, transfer rice to breakfast bowls and serve right away.

RICE PUDDING

Preparation Time: 20 minutes

Servings: 6

Ingredients:

7 oz. long grain rice

- 1 tbsp. butter
- 4 oz. water

- 16 oz. milk
- 3 oz. sugar
- one egg
- 1 tbsp. cream
- 1 tsp. vanilla
- A pinch of salt
- Cinnamon to the taste

Directions:

1. Put the butter in your instant pot, set it on Sauté mode; melt it, add rice and stir.
2. Add water and milk and stir again
3. Add salt and sugar, stir again, close the lid and cook at High for 8 minutes.
4. Meanwhile, in a bowl, mix cream with vanilla and eggs and stir well
5. Quick release the pressure, carefully open the lid; and pour some of the liquid from the pot over egg mixture and stir very well.
6. Pour this into the pot and whisk well
7. Seal the instant pot lid, cook at High for 10 minutes, release pressure, open the instant pot lid, pour pudding into bowls, sprinkle cinnamon on top and serve

BLACK BEANS AND RICE.

Preparation Time: 35 minutes

Servings: 4

Ingredients:

- 1 cup.onion, diced
- 2 cups.brown rice
- 2 cups.dry black beans

- 4 cloves garlic, crushed and then minced.
- 9 cups.water
- 1 tsp. salt
- 1 to 2 limes, optional
- Avocado, optional

Directions:

1. Put garlic and onion in your Instant Pot
2. Add the black beans and the brown rice. Pour in the water and sprinkle the salt. Close the lid. Press "Manual" and set the time to 28 minutes.
3. When the timer is up, press "Cancel" or unplug the pot. Let the pressure release naturally. You can let it sit for 20 minutes
4. Scoop into a serving bowl and squeeze a lime wedge over the bowl
5. Serve with a couple of avocado slices for garnishing.

CURRY RICE

Preparation Time: 15 minutes

Cooking Time: 4 minutes

Servings: 4

Ingredients:

- 1 ½ cup jasmine rice
- 1 tablespoon curry paste
- ½ cup fresh cilantro, chopped
- 1 tablespoon coconut oil
- ¼ cup almond milk
- 3 cups of water
- 1 teaspoon salt

- 1 tablespoon pine nuts

Directions:

1. Mix up together almond milk, salt, and curry paste.
2. Place jasmine rice in the instant pot bowl. Add almond milk mixture.
3. Then add coconut oil, water, and pine nuts.
4. Mix the mixture up until homogenous.
5. Close and seal the lid. Set High-pressure mode and cook rice for 4 minutes.
6. Then allow natural pressure release for 10 minutes.
7. Season cooked curry rice with cilantro.

Nutrition Values: Calories 344, fat 10.7, fiber 3.5, carbs 56.2, protein 5.4

TACO PASTA

Preparation Time: 10 minutes

Cooking Time: 5 minutes

Servings: 5

Ingredients:

- 15 oz pasta
- 4 cups of water
- 1 teaspoon salt
- 1 tablespoon almond butter
- 1 tablespoon Taco seasoning
- ¼ cup of coconut yogurt

Directions:

1. Pour water in the instant pot bowl. Add pasta and salt.

2. Close and seal the lid. Set High-pressure mode and cook pasta for 3 minutes. Use quick pressure release.
3. Then open the lid, add almond butter, Taco seasoning, yogurt, and mix up the pasta well.
4. Close the lid and saute it for 1 minute more.
5. Stir the cooked meal before serving.

Nutrition Values: Calories 271, fat 3.8, fiber 0.3, carbs 48.5, protein 10.4

CAPRESE PASTA

Preparation Time: 10 minutes

Cooking Time: 10 minutes

Servings: 4

Ingredients:

- 9 oz pasta
- 3 cups vegetable broth
- 1 cup fresh basil
- ½ cup tomatoes, chopped
- 1 teaspoon salt
- ½ teaspoon ground black pepper
- 1 onion, diced
- 1 tablespoon olive oil
- 4 oz firm tofu, chopped
- 4 oz vegan Parmesan, grated

Directions:

1. Set Saute mode and pour olive oil.
2. Add ½ cup of fresh basil and onion. Saute the ingredients for 5 minutes. Stir from time to time.
3. Then add salt, chopped tomatoes, ground black pepper, and pasta. Mix

up the mixture carefully.

4. Add remaining basil. Close the lid. Set Pressure mode and cook for 5 minutes.

5. Then use quick pressure release.

6. Open the lid and add tofu and cheese and Parmesan.

7. Mix up the pasta well before serving.

Nutrition Values: Calories 366, fat 7.3, fiber 1.3, carbs 45.6, protein 25.5

PIZZA PASTA

Preparation Time: 10 minutes

Cooking Time: 6 minutes

Servings: 4

Ingredients:

- 1 cup pizza sauce

- 1 cup macaroni

- 2 cups spaghetti sauce

- 1 teaspoon salt

- 6 oz vegan Cheddar cheese, grated

- 5 oz firm tofu, crumbled

- 1 teaspoon Italian seasoning

- 4 corn tortillas, chopped

Directions:

1. Pour pizza sauce in the instant pot.

2. Add the layer of macaroni and sprinkle it with salt.

3. After this, add Italian seasoning and spaghetti sauce.

4. Close the lid and cook meal for 5 minutes on Manual mode (high pressure).

5. Use quick pressure release and open the lid.

6. Mix up the mixture, add grated Cheddar cheese and crumbled tofu. Mix up well.

7. Then add chopped tortillas and close the lid.

8. Cook it on High for 1 minute more. Use quick pressure release. Mix up the cooked meal gently.

Nutrition Values: Calories 359, fat 15.7, fiber 6.5, carbs 50.1, protein 10

PASTA ALFREDO

Preparation Time: 10 minutes

Cooking Time: 10 minutes

Servings: 4

Ingredients:

- 12 oz spaghetti

- 3 cups vegetable broth

- 1 teaspoon salt

- 1 teaspoon minced garlic

- 1 cup cauliflower, chopped

- 1 cup of water

- ½ cup cashew, chopped

- 1 teaspoon coconut oil

Directions:

1. Place coconut oil and minced garlic in the instant pot.

2. Add salt, cashew, and cauliflower.

3. Then add water and close the lid. Cook it on High pressure for 4 minutes.

4. Use the quick pressure release, open

the lid and transfer the mixture in the blender.

5. Blend it until smooth.

6. After this, add vegetable broth and spaghetti in the instant pot. Close and seal the lid.

7. Cook it on High pressure for 5 minutes (quick pressure release).

8. Drain the vegetable broth and transfer spaghetti in the bowls.

9. Pour the cauliflower Alfredo sauce over the spaghetti and serve it warm.

Nutrition Values: Calories 389, fat 12.1, fiber 1.2, carbs 54.4, protein 16.4

PENNE RIGATE

Preparation Time: 10 minutes

Cooking Time: 20 minutes

Servings: 2

Ingredients:

- 8 oz penne pasta
- 1 teaspoon tomato paste
- 1 teaspoon salt
- 3 cups vegetable broth
- 1 onion, diced
- ½ zucchini, chopped
- 1 tablespoon olive oil
- ¼ cup mushrooms, chopped
- ¼ teaspoon minced garlic
- 1 teaspoon dried oregano

Directions:

1. Pour olive oil in the instant pot.

2. Add salt, diced onion, zucchini, and

mushrooms.

3. Then add dried oregano and minced garlic. Stir it carefully and saute for 15 minutes.

4. After this, add tomato paste, vegetable broth, and penne pasta. Mix it up and close the lid.

5. Seal the lid and set Manual mode (high pressure).

6. Cook pasta for 4 minutes. Use the quick pressure release.

7. Open the lid and mix up the meal carefully before serving.

Nutrition Values: Calories 481, fat 1.9, fiber 2.3, carbs 71.6, protein 21.8

DILL ORZO

Preparation Time: 10 minutes

Cooking Time: 10 minutes

Servings: 3

Ingredients:

- 1 cup orzo
- 1 ½ cup water
- 1 teaspoon salt
- 1 teaspoon dried dill
- 1 teaspoon coconut oil
- 1 tomato, chopped

Directions:

1. Toss coconut oil in the instant pot and melt it on Saute mode.

2. Add orzo, salt, dried dill, and chopped tomato. Mix it up and saute for 5 minutes.

3. After this, add water and close the lid. Seal it.

4. Set Manual mode (High pressure) and cook orzo for 5 minutes.

5. Use quick pressure release. Open the lid and mix up the cooked orzo carefully.

Nutrition Values: Calories 230, fat 2.6, fiber 2.3, carbs 43.4, protein 7.3

TOMATO FARFALLE WITH ARUGULA

Preparation Time: 10 minutes

Cooking Time: 4 minutes

Servings: 3

Ingredients:

- 1 cup farfalle
- ½ cup arugula
- ¼ teaspoon garlic, diced
- ½ cup cherry tomatoes, halved
- 4 oz vegan Parmesan, grated
- 1/3 cup walnuts, chopped
- 4 tablespoon olive oil
- 3 cups of water

Directions:

1. Pour water in the instant pot bowl and add farfalle. Close and seal the lid.

2. Cook farfalle on Manual mode (High pressure) for 4 minutes. Then use quick pressure release.

3. Drain water from the farfalle.

4. After this, in the food processor blend together garlic, arugula, vegan cheese, walnuts, and olive oil.

5. When the mixture is smooth, transfer it over the farfalle. Mix up well.

6. Transfer the cooked meal on the plates and garnish with cherry tomato halves.

Nutrition Values: Calories 636, fat 28.3, fiber 4, carbs 66.6, protein 28.5

BUCKWHEAT GROATS

Preparation Time: 10 minutes

Cooking Time: 15 minutes

Servings: 2

Ingredients:

- 1 cup buckwheat groats
- 1 teaspoon dried dill
- 1 carrot, grated
- 1 tablespoon olive oil
- 1 teaspoon salt
- 2 cups of water

Directions:

1. Pour olive oil in the instant pot and add grated carrot. Saute it for 10 minutes. Stir it from time to time.

2. Then add buckwheat groats, dried dill, and salt.

3. Add water, close and seal the lid.

4. Set Manual mode (High pressure) and cook buckwheat for 4 minutes.

5. Use quick pressure release and open the lid.

6. Mix up the buckwheat groats and transfer into the serving bowls.

Nutrition Values: Calories 275, fat 8.9, fiber 6.8, carbs 45.6, protein 7.9

CREAMY SPELT BERRIES

Preparation Time: 5 minutes

Cooking Time: 25 minutes

Servings: 4

Ingredients:

- 1 cup spelt berries, unsoaked
- 1 teaspoon coconut oil
- 1 teaspoon salt
- 1 ½ cup vegetable broth

Directions:

1. Put spelt berries, coconut oil, salt, and vegetable broth in the instant pot bowl.
2. Close the lid and set Manual mode (high pressure).
3. Seal the lid and cook meal for 25 minutes.
4. Then use quick pressure release.
5. Open the lid and stir it gently before serving.

Nutrition Values: Calories 182, fat 2.4, fiber 5.5, carbs 33.1, protein 5.2

BULGUR SALAD

Preparation Time: 10 minutes

Cooking Time: 10 minutes

Servings: 3

Ingredients:

- 1/3 cup bulgur
- 1 cup of water
- 1 teaspoon salt
- 1 teaspoon tomato paste
- 1 onion, diced
- 1 bell pepper, chopped
- ½ cup tomatoes
- ½ cup arugula, chopped
- 1 teaspoon olive oil

Directions:

1. Pour olive oil in the instant pot. Add bell pepper and diced onion.
2. Mix up the vegetables and saute for 3-4 minutes.
3. After this, add bulgur, tomato paste, salt, and water. Mix it up carefully.
4. Close the lid and cook the meal on High for 4 minutes. Then use quick pressure release.
5. Meanwhile, in the salad bowl, mix up together chopped tomatoes and arugula.
6. When the bulgur is cooked, open the lid and chill it till the room temperature.
7. Add chilled bulgur in the salad bowl and mix up well.

Nutrition Values: Calories 102, fat 2, fiber 4.7, carbs 19.9, protein 3.1

VEGAN QUINOA PILAF

Preparation Time: 10 minutes

Cooking Time: 1 minute

Servings: 6

Ingredients:

- 3 cups quinoa
- 3 cups vegetable broth
- 1 teaspoon salt

- 1 teaspoon dried dill
- 1 teaspoon dried cilantro
- 1 garlic clove, peeled
- 1 teaspoon turmeric
- 1 teaspoon onion powder
- 1 tablespoon almond butter
- ¼ cup fresh parsley, chopped

Directions:

1. Mix up together salt, dried dill, cilantro, turmeric, and onion powder.
2. In the instant pot combine together dill mixture with quinoa.
3. Add garlic clove, almond butter, and vegetable broth.
4. Close and seal the lid.
5. Set Manual mode for 1 minute (High pressure) and cook quinoa.
6. When the time is over, use quick pressure release.
7. Open the lid, transfer the cooked quinoa in the bowls and sprinkle with fresh parsley.

Nutrition Values: Calories 353, fat 7.4, fiber 6.4, carbs 56.5, protein 15.2

RICE GARDEN SALAD

Preparation Time: 10 minutes

Cooking Time: 6 minutes

Servings: 4

Ingredients:

- 1 cup of rice
- 2 cups of water
- 1 teaspoon salt

- ½ cup spinach, chopped
- 1 cucumber, chopped
- ½ cup tomatoes, chopped
- 1 tablespoon olive oil
- 1 teaspoon chili flakes
- ½ cup green peas, canned
- 1 tablespoon fresh dill, chopped

Directions:

1. Cook rice: place it in the instant pot, add salt and water. Close and seal the lid. Set manual mode (high pressure) for 6 minutes.
2. When the time is over, use quick pressure release.
3. Meanwhile, in the salad bowl mix up together chopped spinach, cucumber, tomatoes, chili flakes, olive oil, dill, and green peas.
4. When the rice is cooked, chill it till room temperature and transfer in the salad bowl.
5. Mix up the salad carefully and serve it warm.

Nutrition Values: Calories 232, fat 4.1, fiber 2.4, carbs 43.8, protein 5.3

LEMON PASTA

Preparation Time: 15 minutes

Cooking Time: 15 minutes

Servings: 4

Ingredients:

- 1 cup almond milk
- ½ lemon
- 12 oz spaghetti

- 3 cups of water
- 1 teaspoon wheat flour
- 1 teaspoon salt
- 1 teaspoon ground black pepper
- 1 teaspoon almond butter
- 1 tablespoon cashew, chopped
- 1 teaspoon fresh basil

Directions:

1. Cook spaghetti: place it in the instant pot bowl, add water and salt.
1. Close and seal the lid and cook on Manual (high pressure) for 4 minutes. Then use quick pressure release.
2. Drain the water and transfer spaghetti in the big bowl.
3. After this, pour almond milk in the instant pot bowl.
4. Add wheat flour, ground black pepper, and juice from ½ lemon.
5. Stir it gently and cook on Saute mode for 10 minutes. Stir it constantly.
6. When the liquid starts to be thick, add cooked spaghetti and mix up well.
7. Switch off the instant pot and close the lid.
8. Let the pasta rest for 2-3 minutes or until it is serving time. Garnish spaghetti with chopped cashew.

Nutrition Values: Calories 426, fat 19.6, fiber 2.1, carbs 52.9, protein 12.4

KIDNEY BEAN DINNER

Preparation Time: 5-8 min.

Cooking Time: 25 min.

Servings: 4

Ingredients:

- 2 roasted peppers, cut to make strips
- 1 teaspoon ground cumin
- 1/2 teaspoon mustard powder
- 1 pound dried red kidney beans
- 1/2 cup shallots, chopped
- 2 cloves garlic, chopped
- 1 teaspoon celery seeds
- Sea salt and ground black pepper, to taste
- 2 cups roasted vegetable broth

Directions:

1. Take your Instant Pot; open the top lid and plug it on.
2. Add the ingredients; gently stir to combine.
3. Properly close the top lid; make sure that safety valve is properly locked.
4. Press "BEAN/CHILI" cooking function; set timer to 25 minutes. Then, set pressure level to "HIGH".
5. Allow the pressure to build to cook the ingredients.
6. After cooking time is over press "CANCEL" setting. Find and press "NPR" for natural pressure release; it takes around 10 minutes to slowly release pressure.
7. Open the top lid, divide the cooked recipe in serving containers. Serve warm.

Nutrition Values:

Calories: 394

Fat: 4g

Saturated Fat: 0g

Trans Fat: 0g

Carbohydrates: 54g

Fiber: 21g

Sodium: 286mg

Protein: 31g

RICE LENTIL MEAL

Preparation Time: 5-8 min.

Cooking Time: 15 min.

Servings: 5-6

Ingredients:

- 1 cup lentils, soaked overnight
- 1 yellow onion, finely chopped
- 1 celery stalk, finely chopped
- 1 tablespoon extra-virgin olive oil
- 1 cup arborio rice
- Black pepper and salt to the taste
- 1 tablespoon parsley, finely chopped
- 3 ¼ cup veggie stock
- 2 garlic cloves, crushed

Directions:

1. Take your Instant Pot; open the top lid and plug it on.
2. Press "SAUTE" cooking function; add the oil and heat it.
3. In the pot, add the onions; stir-cook using wooden spatula until turns translucent and softened for 3-4 minutes.
4. Add the celery and parsley, stir-cook for 1 minute.
5. Add the garlic, rice, stock, and lentils; stir the mix.
6. Properly close the top lid; make sure that safety valve is properly locked.
7. Press "MANUAL" cooking function; set timer to 10 minutes. Then, set pressure level to "HIGH".
8. Allow the pressure to build to cook the ingredients.
9. After cooking time is over press "CANCEL" setting. Find and press "NPR" for natural pressure release; it takes around 10 minutes to slowly release pressure.
10. Open the top lid, divide the cooked recipe in serving containers. Serve warm.

Nutrition Values:

Calories: 193

Fat: 4g

Saturated Fat: 1g

Trans Fat: 0g

Carbohydrates: 35g

Fiber: 4g

Sodium: 428mg

Protein: 6g

MUSHROOM QUINOA PILAF

Preparation Time: 5-8 min.

Cooking Time: 5-7 min.

Servings: 4

Ingredients:

- 1 onion, chopped
- 1 bell pepper, chopped
- 2 garlic cloves, chopped

- 2 cups dry quinoa
- 3 cups water
- 2 tablespoons olive oil
- 2 cups Cremini mushrooms, thinly sliced
- 1/3 teaspoon ground black pepper, or more to taste
- 1 teaspoon cayenne pepper
- 1/2 teaspoon sea salt
- 1/2 teaspoon dried dill
- 1/4 teaspoon ground bay leaf

Directions:

1. Take your Instant Pot; open the top lid and plug it on.
2. Add the water and quinoa; gently stir to combine.
3. Properly close the top lid; make sure that safety valve is properly locked.
4. Press "MANUAL" cooking function; set timer to 1 minute. Then, set pressure level to "HIGH".
5. Allow the pressure to build to cook the ingredients.
6. After cooking time is over press "CANCEL" setting. Find and press "NPR" for natural pressure release; it takes around 10 minutes to slowly release pressure.
7. Drain quinoa and set it aside.
8. Press "SAUTE" cooking function; add the oil and heat it.
9. In the pot, add the onions; stir-cook using wooden spatula until turns translucent and softened.
10. Add the bell pepper, garlic, and mushrooms; stir-cook for 1-2 minutes.
11. Add the mix in a bowl; mix in the quinoa and other ingredients. Serve fresh.

Nutrition Values:

Calories: 386

Fat: 12g

Saturated Fat: 2g

Trans Fat: 0g

Carbohydrates: 58g

Fiber: 16g

Sodium: 284mg

Protein: 14g

CABBAGE RICE TREAT

Preparation Time: 5-8 min.

Cooking Time: 10 min.

Servings: 4

Ingredients:

- 1 head purple cabbage, cut to make wedges
- 2 ripe tomatoes, pureed
- 2 tablespoons tomato ketchup
- 2 tablespoons olive oil
- 2 shallots, diced
- 1 garlic clove, minced
- 1 bay leaf
- 1/4 teaspoon marjoram
- 1/2 teaspoon cayenne pepper
- 1 cup basmati rice
- 1 ½ cups water
- Salt and freshly ground black pepper,

to taste

- 1/4 cup fresh chives, chopped

Directions:

1. Take your Instant Pot; open the top lid and plug it on.
2. Press "SAUTE" cooking function; add the oil and heat it.
3. In the pot, add the shallots; stir-cook using wooden spatula until turns translucent and softened for 2 minutes.
4. Add the minced garlic and cook until it is lightly browned.
5. Add the cabbage, tomatoes, ketchup, rice, water, bay leaf, marjoram, cayenne pepper, salt, and black pepper; stir the mix.
6. Properly close the top lid; make sure that safety valve is properly locked.
7. Press "MANUAL" cooking function; set timer to 6 minutes. Then, set pressure level to "HIGH".
8. Allow the pressure to build to cook the ingredients.
9. After cooking time is over press "CANCEL" setting. Find and press "NPR" for natural pressure release; it takes around 10 minutes to slowly release pressure.
10. Open the top lid, divide the cooked recipe in serving containers. Top with the chives. Serve warm.

Nutrition Values:

Calories: 257

Fat: 13g

Saturated Fat: 2g

Trans Fat: 0g

Carbohydrates: 34g

Fiber: 11g

Sodium: 354mg

Protein: 9g

ALMOND QUINOA PILAF

Preparation Time: 5-8 min.

Cooking Time: 8 min.

Servings: 4

Ingredients:

- 1 tablespoon vegan butter or vegetable oil
- 14 ounces canned veggie stock
- 1 celery stalk, finely chopped
- ½ cup yellow onion, finely chopped
- 1 ½ cups quinoa, washed and drained
- Salt to the taste
- ¼ cup water
- 2 tablespoons parsley leaves, chopped
- ½ cup almonds, sliced and toasted

Directions:

1. Take your Instant Pot; open the top lid and plug it on.
2. Press "SAUTE" cooking function; add the oil or butter and heat it.
3. In the pot, add the onions, celery; stir-cook using wooden spatula until turns translucent and softened for 4-5 minutes.
4. Add the stock, water, quinoa, and salt, stir the mix.
5. Properly close the top lid; make sure

that safety valve is properly locked.

6. Press "MANUAL" cooking function; set timer to 3 minutes. Then, set pressure level to "HIGH".

7. Allow the pressure to build to cook the ingredients.

8. After cooking time is over press "CANCEL" setting. Find and press "NPR" for natural pressure release; it takes around 10 minutes to slowly release pressure.

9. Open the top lid, divide the cooked recipe in serving containers. Top with the almond and parsley. Serve warm.

Nutrition Values:

Calories: 176

Fat: 6g

Saturated Fat: 0.3g

Trans Fat: 0g

Carbohydrates: 15g

Fiber: 3g

Sodium: 142mg

Protein: 7g

BEAN PEPPER SALAD

Preparation Time: 5-8 min.

Cooking Time: 30 min.

Servings: 3-4

Ingredients:

- 1 red bell pepper, seeded and chopped

- 1 green bell pepper, seeded and chopped

- 1 teaspoon ground sumac

- 1 1/2 cup mix of black beans and Northern beans

- 6 cups water

- 1 cucumber, peeled and sliced

- 3 tablespoons extra-virgin olive oil

- 1 tablespoon fresh lime juice

- 1/4 cup fresh parsley leaves, roughly chopped

- 1/4 teaspoon freshly ground black pepper

- 1/2 teaspoon red pepper flakes

- Salt, to taste

Directions:

1. Take your Instant Pot; open the top lid and plug it on.

2. Add the water and beans; gently stir to combine.

3. Properly close the top lid; make sure that safety valve is properly locked.

4. Press "BEAN/CHILI" cooking function; set timer to 30 minutes. Then, set pressure level to "HIGH".

5. Allow the pressure to build to cook the ingredients.

6. After cooking time is over press "CANCEL" setting. Find and press "NPR" for natural pressure release; it takes around 10 minutes to slowly release pressure.

7. Drain the beans and add in a mixing bowl.

8. Mix in the other ingredients and serve fresh or chilled.

Nutrition Values:

Calories: 210

Fat: 5g

Saturated Fat: 1g

Trans Fat: 0g

Carbohydrates: 31g

Fiber: 8g

Sodium: 154mg

Protein: 10g

LENTILS TOMATO BOWL

Preparation Time: 5-8 min.

Cooking Time: 12 min.

Servings: 4

Ingredients:

- 1 teaspoon garlic, minced
- 1 teaspoon turmeric powder
- Sea salt and ground black pepper, to taste
- 1 teaspoon sweet paprika
- 1 tablespoon olive oil
- 2 cups red lentils
- 1/2 cup scallions, finely chopped
- 1 (15-ounce) can tomatoes, crushed
- 1 bay leaf
- 1 handful fresh cilantro leaves, chopped

Directions:

1. Take your Instant Pot; open the top lid and plug it on.
2. Add the olive oil, lentils, scallions, garlic, turmeric, salt, black pepper, paprika, tomatoes, and bay leaf; gently stir to combine.
3. Properly close the top lid; make sure that safety valve is properly locked.

4. Press "MANUAL" cooking function; set timer to 12 minutes. Then, set pressure level to "HIGH".
5. Allow the pressure to build to cook the ingredients.
6. After cooking time is over press "CANCEL" setting. Find and press "NPR" for natural pressure release; it takes around 10 minutes to slowly release pressure.
7. Open the top lid, remove the bay leaf, divide the cooked recipe in serving containers. Top with some cilantro. Serve warm.

Nutrition Values:

Calories: 396

Fat: 5g

Saturated Fat: 1g

Trans Fat: 0g

Carbohydrates: 58g

Fiber: 14g

Sodium: 536mg

Protein: 24g

SQUASH BARLEY MEAL

Preparation Time: 5-8 min.

Cooking Time: 43 min.

Servings: 4

Ingredients:

- 1/2 cup scallions, chopped
- 2 cups butternut squash, peeled and cubed
- 1/2 teaspoon turmeric powder
- 2 tablespoons olive oil divided
- 2 cloves garlic, minced

- 2 cups barley, whole
- 4 ½ cups water
- Sea salt and ground black pepper, to taste

Directions:

1. Take your Instant Pot; open the top lid and plug it on.
2. Press "SAUTE" cooking function; add the oil and heat it.
3. In the pot, add the garlic, scallions; stir-cook using wooden spatula until turns translucent and softened.
4. Add the ingredients; gently stir to combine.
5. Properly close the top lid; make sure that safety valve is properly locked.
6. Press "MANUAL" cooking function; set timer to 40 minutes. Then, set pressure level to "HIGH".
7. Allow the pressure to build to cook the ingredients.
8. After cooking time is over press "CANCEL" setting. Find and press "NPR" for natural pressure release; it takes around 10 minutes to slowly release pressure.
9. Open the top lid, divide the cooked recipe in serving containers. Serve warm.

Nutrition Values:

Calories: 356

Fat: 6g

Saturated Fat: 1g

Trans Fat: 0g

Carbohydrates: 62g

Fiber: 18g

Sodium: 426mg

Protein: 9g

CREAMED PEAS & RICE

Preparation Time: 5-8 min.

Cooking Time: min.

Servings: 3

Ingredients:

- 4 ounces fresh green peas
- 2 fresh green chilies, chopped
- 1 garlic clove, pressed
- 1 cup basmati rice, rinsed
- 1 ¼ cups water
- Kosher salt and white pepper, to taste
- 2 tablespoons fresh coriander
- 1/2 cup small onions, chopped
- 4 whole cloves
- 1/2 cup coconut cream
- 1 tablespoon fresh lime juice

Directions:

1. Take your Instant Pot; open the top lid and plug it on.
2. Add the ingredients except for the lime juice; gently stir to combine.
3. Properly close the top lid; make sure that safety valve is properly locked.
4. Press "MANUAL" cooking function; set timer to 4-6 minutes. Then, set pressure level to "HIGH".
5. Allow the pressure to build to cook the ingredients.
6. After cooking time is over press "CANCEL" setting. Find and press "NPR" for natural pressure release; it

takes around 10 minutes to slowly release pressure.

7. Open the top lid, mix in the lime juice, divide the cooked recipe in serving containers. Serve warm.

Nutrition Values:

Calories: 326

Fat: 16g

Saturated Fat: 3g

Trans Fat: 0g

Carbohydrates: 43g

Fiber: 8g

Sodium: 346mg

Protein: 9g

CORNMEAL ONION POLENTA

Preparation Time: 5-8 min.

Cooking Time: 12 min.

Servings: 3

Ingredients:

- 2 cups hot water
- 2 teaspoons garlic, minced
- 1 tablespoon chili powder
- 1 cup cornmeal
- 1 bunch green onion, thinly sliced
- 2 cups veggie stock
- Vegetable oil as required
- ¼ cup cilantro, finely chopped
- Black pepper and salt to the taste
- 1 teaspoon cumin
- 1 teaspoon oregano
- A pinch of cayenne pepper
- ½ teaspoon smoked paprika

Directions:

1. Take your Instant Pot; open the top lid and plug it on.

2. Press "SAUTE" cooking function; add the oil and heat it.

3. In the pot, add the onions, garlic; stir-cook using wooden spatula until turns translucent and softened for 2 minutes.

4. Add the stock, hot water, cornmeal, cilantro, salt, pepper, chili powder, cumin, oregano, paprika and a pinch of cayenne pepper; stir the mix.

5. Properly close the top lid; make sure that safety valve is properly locked.

6. Press "MANUAL" cooking function; set timer to 10 minutes. Then, set pressure level to "HIGH".

7. Allow the pressure to build to cook the ingredients.

8. After cooking time is over press "CANCEL" setting. Find and press "NPR" for natural pressure release; it takes around 10 minutes to slowly release pressure.

9. Open the top lid, divide the cooked recipe in serving containers. Serve warm.

Nutrition Values:

Calories: 285

Fat: 2g

Saturated Fat: 0g

Trans Fat: 0g

Carbohydrates: 42g

Fiber: 4g

Sodium: 364mg

Protein: 9g

SOUPS AND STEWS

INSTANT POT VEGGIE SOUP

Servings: 6

Preparation time: 10 minutes

Cooking Time: 35

Ingredients:

- 12 ounces Italian veggies mix, frozen
- 12 ounces California veggies mix, frozen
- 15 ounces canned pinto beans mixed with kidney beans
- 15 ounces canned cannellini beans
- 15 ounces canned tomatoes, chopped
- ¼ cup quinoa
- 1 tablespoon garlic, minced
- 1 tablespoon basil, dry
- 1 tablespoon hot sauce
- ½ tablespoon oregano, dry
- Salt to the taste
- 1 teaspoon onion powder
- 3 cups hot water

Directions:

1. In your instant pot, mix Italian and California veggies with pinto, kidney and cannelloni beans.
2. Add tomatoes, quinoa, basil, oregano, garlic, hot sauce, onion powder, salt to the taste and the hot water.
3. Stir, close the lid and cook on High for 35 minutes.
4. Release pressure naturally, transfer into soup bowls and serve right away.
5. Enjoy!

Nutrition Values: Calories 192, fat 1, carbs 34, fiber 11.2, protein 10.5

LENTILS SOUP

Servings: 8

Preparation time: 15 minutes

Cooking Time: 10 minutes

Ingredients:

- 8 cups veggie stock
- 2 cups green lentils
- 1 and ½ pounds red potatoes, cubed
- 1 yellow onion, chopped
- 8 ounces mushrooms, cut in quarters
- 2 carrots, sliced
- Salt and pepper to the taste
- 2 celery ribs, chopped
- 2 bay leaves
- 4 garlic cloves, minced
- 2 teaspoons thyme, dry
- 1 tablespoon soy sauce
- 1 teaspoon rosemary, dry
- ½ teaspoon sage, dry

Directions:

1. Put lentils in your instant pot.
2. Add stock, potatoes, mushrooms, onion, carrots, celery, bay leaves, garlic, soy sauce, thyme, rosemary,

sage, salt and pepper, stir everything, cover pot and cook on High for 10 minutes.

3. Release pressure naturally, leave aside for 10 minutes, discard bay leaves, divide soup amongst bowls and serve hot.

4. Enjoy!

Nutrition Values: Calories 180, fat 4.5, carbs 26, fiber 12.4, sugar 2.3, protein 10.4

VEGAN CAULIFLOWER AND SWEET POTATO SOUP

Servings: 8

Preparation time: 10 minutes

Cooking Time: 30 minutes

Ingredients:

- ½ teaspoon cumin seeds
- 3 garlic cloves, minced
- 1 tablespoon ginger paste
- 1 yellow onion, chopped
- 1 chili pepper, minced
- 4 cups veggie stock
- 1 pound sweet potatoes, cut into small cubes
- 1/8 teaspoon cinnamon powder
- 1 tablespoon curry powder
- 1 cauliflower head, florets separated
- 15 ounces canned chickpeas, drained
- 15 ounces canned tomatoes, chopped
- Salt and pepper to the taste
- 3 cups water
- A pinch of cayenne pepper

- 1 tablespoon peanut butter

Directions:

1. Heat up a pan over medium heat, add onions and brown them for 3 minutes.

2. Add ginger, cumin seeds, chili and garlic, stir and cook for 30 seconds more.

3. Pour everything into your instant pot, add potatoes, stock, curry powder and cinnamon, stir, cover and cook on High for 20 minutes.

4. Release pressure naturally, uncover pot, add tomatoes, chickpeas and cauliflower.

5. Add 3 cups water, salt, pepper and cayenne, stir, cover and cook on High for 10 more minutes.

6. Release pressure naturally, add peanut butter, stir, pour into soup bowls and serve hot.

7. Enjoy!

Nutrition Values: Calories 113, fat 1.8, carbs 20, fiber 3.6, sugar 2, protein 5.2

TASTY INSTANT POT TOMATO SOUP

Servings: 4

Preparation time: 15 minutes

Cooking Time: 30 minutes

Ingredients:

- 2 and ½ pounds tomatoes, chopped
- 2 garlic cloves, crushed
- 1 onion, finely chopped
- 1 tablespoon vegan butter
- 1 tablespoon vegetable oil

- 2 thyme sprigs, chopped
- Salt and black pepper to the taste
- 4 ounces veggie stock

Directions:

1. Heat up a pan with the oil and the vegan butter over medium high heat, add garlic and onion, stir and cook for 4 minutes.
2. Transfer this to your instant pot, add tomatoes, stock, salt, pepper and thyme, stir, and cook on High for 5 minutes.
3. Reduce temperature to your instant pot and cook soup for 15 minutes more.
4. Release pressure naturally for 10 minutes, pour the soup into your blender, pulse very well and then strain the soup.
5. Divide amongst serving bowls and serve right away.
6. Enjoy!

Nutrition Values: Calories 130, fat 6, carbs 0, fiber 3, protein 4

DELICIOUS PUMPKIN SOUP

Servings: 12

Preparation time: 15 minutes

Cooking Time: 20 minutes

Ingredients:

- 1 butternut pumpkin, cut into medium chunks
- 1 tablespoon vegan butter
- 4 bay leaves
- 1 yellow onion, chopped

- A pinch of curry powder
- Salt and black pepper to the taste
- 1-quart veggie stock
- 1 potato, chopped
- 1 apple, grated
- 15 ounces coconut milk

Directions:

1. Heat up a pan with the vegan butter over medium high heat, add onion, stir and cook for 3-4 minutes.
2. Transfer to your instant pot and mix with pumpkin, potato, curry powder, salt, pepper, stock and bay leaves.
3. Stir, cook on High for 5 minutes and then release pressure naturally.
4. Add the apple and cook soup on High for 15 minutes more.
5. Release pressure again, discard bay leaves, pour soup into a blender and pulse well.
6. Add coconut milk, pulse again, divide amongst bowls and serve.
7. Enjoy!

Nutrition Values: Calories 130, fat 2, carbs 9, fiber 2, protein 7

INSTANT POT SPLIT PEA SOUP

Servings: 6

Preparation time: 10 minutes

Cooking Time: 15 minutes

Ingredients:

2 and ½ cups veggie stock

1 cup split peas

1 yellow onion, finely chopped

2 carrots, diced

1 potato, chopped

Salt and black pepper to the taste

1 bay leaf

2 small garlic cloves, minced

Some chopped parsley for serving

Directions:

1. In your instant pot, mix onion with split pea, carrots, potato, garlic, bay leaf and stock.

2. Stir, cover pot and cook on High for 15 minutes.

3. Release pressure naturally, discard bay leaf, add salt and pepper to the taste, divide amongst soup bowls and serve with parsley sprinkled on top.

4. Enjoy!

Nutrition Values: Calories 150, fat 0.8, carbs 27, fiber 4.8, protein 9.5

INSTANT POT CREAM OF BROCCOLI   *Good flavor*

Servings: 6   *Needs some texture.*

Preparation time: 10 minutes

Cooking Time: 15 minutes

Ingredients:

- 2 tablespoons coconut oil

- 3 leeks, white parts separated and chopped

- 1 tablespoon curry powder

- 2 shallots, chopped

- 1 and ½ pounds broccoli florets

- Salt and black pepper to the taste

- ¼ cup apple, chopped

- 4 cups veggie stock

- 1 cup coconut milk

- Chopped chives for serving

Directions:

1. Heat up a pan with the oil over medium high heat, add leeks and shallots, stir and cook for 4 minutes.

2. Add curry powder and some ~~salt,~~ stir, cook for 1 minute and pour everything in your instant pot.

3. Add broccoli, stock, ~~salt and pepper to the taste,~~ cover and cook on High for 10 minutes.   *S & P @ the end*

4. Release pressure naturally, add apple and cook on High for 5 minutes more.

5. Release pressure again, pour the soup into your blender and pulse well until you obtain cream.   *→ leave a little chunky*

6. Add more salt and pepper if needed and the coconut milk and blend again.

7. Divide amongst soup bowls, sprinkle chives on top and serve.

8. Enjoy!

Nutrition Values: Calories 260, fat 14, carbs 24, fiber 5, sugar 3.5, protein 13

INSTANT POT BEETS SOUP (BORSCHT)

Servings: 4

Preparation time: 10 minutes

Cooking Time: 45 minutes

Ingredients:

- 8 cups beets, peeled and chopped

- 1 cup water

- 2 carrots, chopped
- 3 celery stalks, chopped
- 1 yellow onion, chopped
- Salt and black pepper to the taste
- 2 garlic cloves, minced
- 3 cups cabbage, shredded
- 1 bay leaf
- ½ tablespoon thyme, dry
- 6 cups veggie stock
- ¼ cup dill, finely chopped
- ½ cup coconut yogurt

Directions:

1. Put the beets in your instant pot, add 1 cup water, cook on High for 7 minutes, release pressure and transfer beets to a bowl filled with ice water.

2. Return the beets to your instant pot, add stock, celery, carrots, onions, garlic, salt, pepper, thyme, cabbage and bay leaf, stir and cook for 45 minutes.

3. Release pressure naturally, discard bay leaf, divide soup amongst bowls and serve with chopped dill sprinkled and with coconut yogurt on top.

4. Enjoy!

Nutrition Values: Calories 110, fat 4, carbs 7, fiber 2, sugar 2, protein 3

POTATO SOUP

Servings: 3

Preparation time: 5 minutes

Cooking Time: 5 minutes

Ingredients:

- 7 potatoes, roughly chopped
- ¼ cup yellow onion, finely chopped
- 1 cup veggie stock
- 1 cup soy milk
- 1 tablespoon chickpea miso
- Salt and white pepper to the taste

Directions:

1. In your instant pot, mix potatoes with onion and stock, stir and cook on High for 5 minutes.

2. Release pressure, add salt, pepper to the taste and miso, cover pot and cook on High for another 5 minutes.

3. Release pressure naturally this time, transfer soup to your blender, add soymilk and pulse well.

4. Divide amongst soup bowls and serve.

5. Enjoy!

Nutrition Values: Calories 260, fat 4.7, carbs 30, fiber 6, sugar 2, protein 6.4

INSTANT POT BLACK BEAN SOUP

Servings: 8

Preparation time: 10 minutes

Cooking Time: 40 minutes

Ingredients:

- 1 pound black beans, soaked and drained
- 1 yellow onion, chopped
- 1 green bell pepper, chopped
- 1 red bell pepper, chopped
- 14 ounces canned tomatoes, chopped

- 3 celery stalks, chopped
- Salt and black pepper to the taste
- 1 tablespoon sweet paprika
- 1 teaspoon hot sauce
- 2 tablespoons cumin
- 6 cups veggie stock
- 2 bay leaves
- 2 tablespoons chili powder
- 1 avocado, chopped for serving
- Tortilla chips for serving
- Chopped cilantro, for serving

Directions:

1. In your instant pot, mix black beans, with stock, onion, red and green bell peppers, celery, tomatoes, salt, pepper, paprika, hot sauce, cumin, chili powder and bay leaves.

2. Stir, cover and cook on High for 40 minutes.

3. Release pressure naturally, discard bay leaves, add more salt and pepper if needed, divide soup amongst bowls, sprinkle cilantro, top with avocado pieces and serve with tortilla chips.

4. Enjoy!

Nutrition Values: Calories 240, fat 2.5, carbs 40, fiber 9, protein 12

COLORFUL SPRING CHILI

Preparation Time: 15 Minutes

Servings: 4

Ingredients:

- 1 cup fennel bulb, sliced
- 1 cup sliced carrots
- 2 radishes, trimmed, sliced
- 8oz. can cannellini beans, rinsed
- ¼ cup onion, chopped
- 2 tablespoon shallots, chopped
- 2 cloves garlic, chopped
- 6 cherry tomatoes, quartered
- ¼ cup chopped celery
- 1 cup tomato paste
- ½ cup vegetable juice
- 1 medium zucchini, cubed
- ½ cup corn kernels
- 1 teaspoon chipotle powder
- ½ teaspoon cumin
- 1 teaspoon dried oregano
- 1 pinch rosemary
- 1 pinch cayenne
- Salt and pepper, to taste

Directions:

1. Combine all ingredients, into the Instant pot, except the zucchinis, corn, and cherry tomatoes.

2. Lock the lid and high-pressure 8 minutes.

3. Use a natural pressure release, then release any remaining pressure with a quick-pressure release method.

4. Stir in reserved zucchinis, corn, and tomatoes. Lock the lid, and high-pressure 1 minute.

5. Perform a quick-pressure release and open the lid.

6. Serve warm.

SOUTHERN CHILI

Preparation Time: 10 Minutes

Servings: 4

Ingredients:

- 1 tablespoon olive oil
- ½ cup chopped white onion
- 1 cup chopped red bell pepper
- 1 small squash, peeled, cubed
- 2 cups cubed zucchini
- 1 teaspoon chipotle powder
- 2 cups can black kidney beans, rinsed
- Salt and pepper, to taste
- 2 14oz. can crushed tomatoes
- ¼ cup pickled chili peppers, chopped
- 1 tablespoon ground cumin
- ¼ teaspoon dried oregano

Directions:

1. Heat oil in Instant pot on Sauté.
2. Add onion and cook 3 minutes.
3. Add spices and cook 2 minutes.
4. Stir in remaining ingredients, and lock the lid.
5. High-pressure 5 minutes.
6. Use a quick-pressure release method.
7. Stir gently and serve.

FAKE CHICKEN CHILI

Preparation Time: 10 Minutes

Servings: 4

Ingredients:

- 1 tablespoon olive oil
- 1 red bell pepper, seeded, chopped
- shredded seitan
- 1 small brown onion, chopped
- 2 cloves garlic, minced
- 14oz. can black beans, rinsed
- 3 cups can crushed tomatoes, with juices
- 1 tablespoon raw cider vinegar
- 1 tablespoon chili powder
- 1 teaspoon chili flakes
- 1 teaspoon dried oregano
- ½ cup vegetable juice
- Salt and pepper, to taste
- 2 cups vegetable stock

Directions:

1. Heat oil in Instant pot on Sauté.
2. Cook bell pepper and onion for 4 minutes.
3. Add garlic and spices. Cook 30 seconds.
4. Stir in remaining ingredients and lock the lid.
5. High-pressure 6 minutes.
6. Use a quick-pressure release method.
7. Open the lid and stir gently. Adjust the seasonings.
8. Serve warm.

BLACK BEAN DELIGHT CHILI

Preparation Time: 15 Minutes

Servings: 4

Ingredients:

- 1 tablespoon olive oil
- 1 red onion, chopped
- ½ cup shredded carrots
- 1 celery stalk, chopped
- 2 cups vegetable stock
- 14oz. can black beans, rinsed
- 1 tablespoon chili powder
- Salt and pepper, to taste
- 2 teaspoons ground cumin
- ½ teaspoon chili flakes
- 2 teaspoons smoked paprika
- ¼ cup chopped cilantro

Directions:

1. Heat olive oil in Instant pot on Sauté.
2. Add onion, carrots, and celery. Cook, stirring 4 minutes.
3. Add garlic, cumin, chili powder, chili flakes, and smoked paprika.
4. Cook 30 seconds or until fragrant.
5. Add remaining ingredients and season with salt and pepper, to taste.
6. Lock the lid and High-pressure 8 minutes.
7. Use a quick pressure release method.
8. Open the lid and stir gently.
9. Serve warm.

FRAGRANT HOKKAIDO CHILI

Preparation Time: 14 Minutes

Servings: 6

Ingredients:

- 2 tablespoon coconut oil

- 1.5lb. Hokkaido pumpkin, peeled, seeded, cubed
- 14oz. can red kidney beans
- ¼ cup chopped onion
- 2 teaspoons ground cumin
- 1 teaspoon allspice
- 1 tablespoon chili powder
- 1 pinch ground cloves
- 1 teaspoon chili flakes
- 1 ½ cups vegetable stock
- Salt and pepper, to taste

Directions:

1. Heat coconut oil into Instant pot on Sauté.
2. Cook onion 4 minutes.
3. Add spices and cook 20 seconds.
4. Add pumpkin and stir, to coat with the spices.
5. Add remaining ingredients and season to taste with salt and pepper.
6. Lock the lid and high-pressure 6 minutes.
7. Use a quick pressure release method and open the lid.
8. Serve warm.

RED LENTILS CHILI

Preparation Time: 10 Minutes

Servings: 6

Ingredients:

1. 1 tablespoon olive oil
2. 1 brown onion, chopped
3. 1 cup red lentils, picked

4. 2 cloves garlic, chopped

5. 1 cup roasted red bell pepper, seeded, sliced

6. 2 carrots, sliced

7. 2 celery stalks, sliced

8. ¼ cup tomato paste

9. 4 cups vegetable stock

10. 15oz. can crushed tomatoes, with juices

11. 1 ½ tablespoon chili powder

12. 1 teaspoon smoked mesquite powder

13. 1 teaspoon ground cumin

14. 1 teaspoon crushed dried basil

15. Salt and pepper, to taste

Direction:

1. Heat olive oil into Instant pot on Sauté.

2. Add onion, carrots, bell pepper, and celery. Cook 4 minutes.

3. Add garlic and spices. Cook 1 minute.

4. Stir in vegetable stock, and remaining ingredients.

5. Lock the lid and high-pressure 7 minutes.

6. Use a quick-pressure release method.

7. Open the lid and stir gently. Adjust the seasonings before serving.

OKRA BEAN CHILI

Preparation Time: 12 Minutes

Servings: 8

Ingredients:

- 1 tablespoon olive oil

- 1 large onion, chopped

- 15oz. can black beans, rinsed

- 15oz. can white beans, rinsed

- 1 cup corn kernels

- 14oz. can black-eyed peas, rinsed

- 2 14oz. can crushed tomatoes

- 1 cups sliced okra

- 2 red bell peppers, seeded

- 4 cloves garlic

- 2 cups zucchinis, cubed

- 2 cups vegetable stock

- 1 ½ tablespoons chili powder

- 1 teaspoon dried oregano

- 1 teaspoon ground cumin powder

- Salt and pepper, to taste

Directions:

1. Heat oil into Instant Pot.

2. Add onions and bell peppers, Cook 4 minutes.

3. Add garlic and spices. Cook 1 minute.

4. Stir in remaining ingredients and lock the lid.

5. High-pressure at Manual 6 minutes.

6. Use a quick-pressure release method. Open the lid and stir gently.

7. Adjust seasonings before serving.

LIKE A FAJITA CHILI

Preparation Time: 13 Minutes

Servings: 6

Ingredients:

- 1 tablespoon olive oil

- ½ cup chopped onion

- 2 cups mixed bell peppers, sliced
- 15oz. can red kidney beans, rinsed
- 7oz. shredded seitan
- 15oz. fire-roasted tomatoes, crushed
- 2 cups vegetable stock
- 1 teaspoon cayenne pepper
- 1 teaspoon chili powder
- 2 cloves garlic, finely chopped
- 1 teaspoon ground cumin
- 1 teaspoon brown sugar
- Salt and pepper, to taste
- 1 teaspoon dried oregano

Directions:

1. Heat olive oil in Instant pot on Sauté.
2. Add onions and bell peppers, and cook 3 minutes.
3. Add garlic and cook 1 minute or until fragrant.
4. Add seitan and cook 2 minutes.
5. Stir in remaining ingredients and lock lid into place.
6. High-pressure 6 minutes.
7. Use a quick pressure release method.
8. Serve warm.

BURGER" CHILI

Preparation Time: 10 Minutes

Servings: 4

Ingredients:

- 1 tablespoon coconut oil
- ½ cup chopped onion
- 2 cloves garlic, minced

- 1 cup vegetable juice
- ½ cup tomato paste
- ½ cup water
- 12oz. veggie burger crumbles
- 2 tablespoons wine vinegar
- 2 teaspoons chili powder
- 1 tablespoon raw cocoa powder
- 1 tablespoon Taco seasoning
- Salt and pepper, to taste
- 1lb. cooked spaghetti
- 2 spring onions, sliced, to serve with

Directions:

1. Heat olive oil in Instant pot on Sauté.
2. Add onions and cook 4 minutes.
3. Add garlic and cook 1 minute.
4. Stir in remaining ingredients, except spaghetti.
5. Lock lid into place and high-pressure 3 minutes.
6. Use a natural pressure release.
7. Serve the chili over cooked spaghetti and top with green onions.

VEGAN CARNE

Preparation Time: 8 Minutes

Servings: 4

Ingredients:

- 1 tablespoon olive oil
- ¼ cup chopped onion
- 2 cups vegetable stock
- 2 red bell peppers, seeded, diced
- Salt and pepper, to taste

- 15oz. can black beans, rinsed, drained
- 1 tablespoon chili powder
- 4 ripe tomatoes, chopped
- 1 tablespoon raw cider vinegar
- 1 teaspoon dried oregano
- 12oz. vegan burger, crumbled
- 1 tablespoon tomato paste
- 2 teaspoons ground cumin

Directions:

1. Heat olive oil into Instant Pot.
2. Add onions and bell peppers. Cook 5 minutes.
3. Add garlic and spices. Cook 1 minute.
4. Stir in remaining ingredients and lock lid into place.
5. High-pressure on Manual 4 minutes.
6. Use a quick-pressure release method.
7. Serve warm.

WHITE BEAN TOMATO CHILI

Preparation Time: 10 Minutes

Servings: 4

Ingredients:

- 1 tablespoon olive oil
- 2 cloves garlic, minced
- ½ teaspoon chipotle powder
- 1 tablespoon smoked paprika
- 15oz. can white beans, rinsed, drained
- 1 green chili pepper, seeded
- 2 cups vegetable stock
- 1 teaspoon ground cumin

- 3 ripe tomatoes, diced
- Salt and pepper, to taste
- 1 teaspoon dried basil
- 1 teaspoon dried marjoram
- 2 cups corn kernels

To top:

- 4 tablespoons cilantro
- 4 tablespoons vegan sour cream, like cashew cream

Directions:

1. Heat oil into Instant pot on Sauté.
2. Add garlic and chili pepper. Cook 1 minute.
3. Add spices and cook 20 seconds.
4. Add remaining ingredients and lock lid into place.
5. High-pressure 4 minutes.
6. Use a quick-pressure release method and open the lid.
7. Sprinkle with cilantro, and divide among bowls. Top with sour cream and serve.

SPICY CHICKPEA CURRY

Preparation Time: 10 Minutes

Servings: 6

Ingredients:

- 4cups cooked chickpeas
- 1(14.5-ounce) can crushed tomatoes
- ¾cup baby green peas
- 1teaspoon ground coriander
- 1tablespoon curry powder
- 2potatoes, peeled, diced

- 1(4-ounce) can minced green chiles, drained
- 1onion, minced
- 3garlic cloves, minced
- ½cup plain vegan yogurt
- ⅓cup minced fresh cilantro leaves
- 1teaspoon ground cumin
- 1½teaspoons grated fresh ginger
- ¼teaspoon cayenne pepper
- 1cup water

Directions:

1. Add all the ingredients except yogurt in your instant pot.
2. Mix well and cover with lid.
3. Cook for about 5 minutes.
4. Add the yogurt and cook for another minute.
5. Serve hot.

CANNELLINI CHILI

Preparation Time: 12 Minutes

Servings: 6

Ingredients:

- 1(16-ounce) can hominy, drained
- 4cups cooked cannellini
- 1potato, peeled and chopped
- 2teaspoons ground coriander
- 1(4-ounce) can minced green chiles, drained
- 1onion, chopped
- 1teaspoon dried marjoram
- ¼teaspoon white pepper

- 4garlic cloves, minced
- 2cups vegetable broth or water
- 2teaspoons ground cumin
- 1teaspoon salt

Directions:

1. Toss the onion, garlic, coriander, cumin and marjoram in an instant pot for 1 minute.
2. Add the chiles, beans, salt, broth, potato, hominy and pepper.
3. Stir well and cover with lid.
4. Cook for 10 minutes.
5. Serve hot.

BROWN RICE & BLACK EYED PEAS CHILI

Preparation Time: 10 Minutes

Servings: 6

Ingredients:

- 3cups cooked black-eyed peas
- ½cup uncooked long-grain brown rice
- 1(28-ounce) can diced tomatoes
- 8ounces tempeh, chopped or crumbled
- 1onion, chopped
- 5garlic cloves, minced
- 1small green bell pepper, seeded and chopped
- 2cups vegetable broth or water
- 2tablespoons chili powder
- 1celery rib, chopped
- 1teaspoon ground cumin

- Salt and black pepper
- 2tablespoons tomato paste
- 1teaspoon dried thyme

Directions:

1. Add the onion, celery, chile, garlic, cumin, chili powder, and tempeh, in an instant pot.
2. Add the tomato paste, all the herbs and the rest of the ingredients.
3. Mix well and add cover using the lid.
4. Cook for about 8 minutes.
5. Serve hot.

CORN, TOMATO & PINTO BEANS CHILI

Preparation Time: 10 Minutes

Servings: 4

Ingredients:

- 2cups corn kernels
- 2tablespoons chili powder
- ½teaspoon ground cumin
- 1tablespoon soy sauce
- 1(24-ounce) jar fire-roasted chunky tomato salsa
- 1cup water
- 3cups cooked pinto beans
- 1teaspoon dried marjoram
- Salt and black pepper

Directions:

1. Add the marjoram, water, cumin, salsa and chili powder in your instant pot.
2. Cover and cook for 1 minute.

3. Add the seasoning, corn, soy sauce and beans.
4. Stir well and cook with the lid on for 5 minutes.
5. Serve hot.

TOMATO FLAVORED CHILI

Preparation Time: 10 Minutes

Servings: 6

Ingredients:

- 3cups cooked dark red kidney beans
- 1(14-ounce) can crushed tomatoes
- 4garlic cloves, minced
- 8ounces seitan
- 3tablespoons tomato paste
- 1(14.5-ounce) can diced fire-roasted tomatoes
- ½teaspoon ground cinnamon
- 2cups water
- 2tablespoons unsweetened cocoa powder
- 1teaspoon salt
- 1tablespoon minced chipotle chiles in adobo
- 2tablespoons almond butter
- 1onion, chopped
- 3tablespoons chili powder
- ½small green bell pepper, seeded and chopped
- ¼teaspoon black pepper

Directions:

1. Add the garlic, vegetables, seasoning, herbs and spices in your instant pot.

2. Add the chipotle chile in adobo, water, tomato paste, roasted tomatoes, crushed tomatoes and butter.

3. Mix well and cover with lid. Cook for about 5 minutes.

4. Add the mixture to a blender and make it smooth.

5. Serve hot.

CREAMY CORN BEAN CHILI

Preparation Time: 10 Minutes

Servings: 4

Ingredients:

- 1cup corn kernels
- 1teaspoon ground coriander
- 1onion, minced
- 2(15-ounce) cans beans, rinsed and drained
- 1tablespoon minced fresh cilantro leaves
- 3tablespoons chili powder
- 1teaspoon ground cumin
- ½cup water
- 3garlic cloves, minced
- ½cup plain unsweetened nondairy milk
- 1small bell pepper (any color), seeded and chopped
- 1cup medium-ground cornmeal
- 4cups cooked dark red kidney beans
- Salt and black pepper
- 2 green chilies, diced
- 1(14-ounce) can crushed tomatoes

- ½teaspoon baking soda
- 1tablespoon soy sauce
- 2teaspoons baking powder
- 2tablespoons olive oil

Directions:

1. In your instant pot add the beans, corn kernel, green chilies, tomatoes, seasoning, oil, soy sauce and the rest of the ingredients.

2. Mix well and cover using the pot's lid.

3. Cook for 8 minutes and serve hot.

SUPREME FALL CHILI

Preparation Time: 15 Minutes

Servings: 6

Ingredients:

- 1 tablespoon olive oil
- 2 cloves garlic, finely chopped
- ¾ cup vegetable stock
- 2 14oz. can fire-roasted tomatoes, crushed
- 2 14oz. can black-eyed beans, rinsed, drained
- 1b. butternut squash, cubed
- 1 onion, chopped
- 1 tablespoon chili powder
- 1 teaspoon ground cumin
- ¼ teaspoon ground nutmeg
- Salt and pepper, to taste

Directions:

1. Heat oil in Instant pot on Sauté.

2. Add onion and cook 3 minutes. Add

garlic to the Instant pot and cook 1 minute.

3. Add spices and cook 20 seconds.

4. Stir in remaining ingredients and lock lid into place.

5. High-pressure 7 minutes.

6. Use a natural pressure release, then perform a quick pressure release to release any remaining pressure.

7. Serve warm.

SEITAN ROAST ROULADE.

Preparation Time: 45 Minutes

Servings: 8

This roast seitan makes an amazing festive or weekend dinner. Just mix up the sides depending on the occasion!

Ingredients:

- 2lbs seitan
- 1 vegan sausage, crumbled or coarsely chopped
- 3 shallots, minced
- 3 garlic cloves, minced
- 2 cups finely minced cremini mushrooms
- 1 (10-ounce) package frozen chopped spinach, thawed and squeezed dry
- 1 jarred roasted red bell pepper, minced
- 1 teaspoon fresh thyme or ½ teaspoon dried thyme
- 1 teaspoon fresh minced sage or ½ teaspoon dried crumbled sage
- 2 teaspoons olive oil
- Salt and freshly ground black pepper

Directions:

1. Warm the oil in the base of your instant pot.

2. Add the shallots and soften for 3 minutes.

3. Add the garlic, mushrooms, thyme, and sage. Cook another 2 minutes.

4. Add the spinach and bell pepper and a little salt and pepper. Cook another 2 minutes.

5. Remove from the heat.

6. Mix with the sausage and set aside.

7. Roll your seitan out onto some 9x12 inch aluminum foil.

8. Spread the stuffing evenly on your seitan and roll it up. Use the foil to seal it. Place in your instant pot steamer basket.

9. Put hot water in your instant pot and lower the steamer basket.

10. Cook on Steam for 30 minutes.

11. Depressurize naturally and serve.

SNACKS

CHICKPEA SLICES

Preparation Time: 10 minutes

Cooking Time: 35 minutes

Servings: 4

Ingredients:

- 4 flour tortillas
- ½ cup chickpeas, soaked
- 2 cups of water
- 1 teaspoon salt
- 1 tablespoon vegan mayonnaise
- 1 bell pepper, chopped

Directions:

1. Place tortillas and chickpeas in the instant pot.
2. Close and seal the lid.
3. Cook the chickpeas on Manual mode for 35 minutes. Use quick pressure release.
4. Drain the water and transfer the chickpeas in the blender.
5. Add salt, vegan mayonnaise, and bell pepper.
6. Blend the mixture.
7. Spread the flour tortillas with the blended chickpeas and roll them.
8. Slice the tortillas into small pieces and secure with toothpicks.

Nutrition Values: Calories 162, fat 3.1, fiber 6.3, carbs 28.4, protein 6.5

CRUNCHY OYSTER MUSHROOMS

Preparation Time: 15 minutes

Cooking Time: 15 minutes

Servings: 3

Ingredients:

- 7 oz oyster mushrooms
- 1 tablespoon olive oil
- 1 teaspoon chili flakes
- ¼ cup bread crumbs
- 1 teaspoon apple cider vinegar
- 1 cup water, for cooking

Directions:

1. Place oyster mushrooms in instant pot pan.
2. Pour water in the instant pot and insert trivet.
3. Place pan with oyster mushrooms on the trivet and close the lid.
4. Seal the lid and cook mushrooms for 10 minutes.
5. After this, use quick pressure release.
6. Open the lid and drain water.
7. Chop the oyster mushrooms roughly and sprinkle with olive oil, chili flakes, and apple cider vinegar.
8. Mix up the mushrooms and let them for 10 minutes to marinate.
9. Then preheat instant pot on Saute mode.
10. Add oyster mushrooms and cook them for 4 minutes.

11. Stir the vegetables and sprinkle with bread crumbs. Mix up the mushrooms well.

12. Transfer them in the serving bowl.

Nutrition Values: Calories 312, fat 5.2, fiber 7.5, carbs 44.3, protein 20.1

JACKFRUIT COATED BITES

Preparation Time: 15 minutes

Cooking Time: 5 minutes

Servings: 4

Ingredients:

- 1 cup jackfruit, canned, drained
- ½ cup wheat flour
- 2 tablespoons soy sauce
- 2 tablespoons maple syrup
- 4 tablespoons agave syrup
- 1 teaspoon ground cumin
- ½ teaspoon salt
- 1 teaspoon paprika
- ½ teaspoon ground black pepper
- 1 teaspoon dried cilantro
- 1 teaspoon turmeric
- ½ cup olive oil

Directions:

1. In the mixing bowl, mix up together soy sauce, maple syrup, agave syrup, ground cumin, salt, and paprika. Whisk the mixture.

2. Place canned jackfruit in the soy mixture and mix up well. Leave it for 10 minutes to marinate.

3. Meanwhile, pour olive oil in the instant pot and preheat it on Saute mode.

4. In the separated bowl, combine together wheat flour, ground black pepper, cilantro, and turmeric.

5. Coat the jackfruit into the wheat mixture.

6. Place the coated pieces of jackfruit in the hot olive oil and cook them for 1 minute from each side or until light brown.

7. Dry the snack with the paper towel and transfer on the serving bowl.

Nutrition Values: Calories 412, fat 257., fiber 1.,6 carbs 47, protein 3

SOFRITAS TOFU

Preparation Time: 5 minutes

Cooking Time: 5 minutes

Servings: 4

Ingredients:

- 8 oz firm tofu, chopped
- ½ teaspoon cayenne pepper
- 1 teaspoon ground black pepper
- 1 teaspoon smoked paprika
- 1 teaspoon chili flakes
- ½ teaspoon salt
- ½ teaspoon brown sugar
- 1 tablespoon avocado oil
- 5 tablespoons vegan Adobo sauce

Directions:

1. Pour avocado oil in the instant pot. Add chopped tofu.

2. Cook it on Saute mode for 1 minute.

3. Sprinkle tofu with cayenne pepper, ground black pepper, smoked paprika, chili flakes, and salt. Mix up well and add sugar.

4. Stir it carefully and cook for 2 minutes.

5. Then add vegan Adobo sauce and mix up the meal well.

6. Cook it for 2 minutes more.

7. Transfer cooked sofritas tofu in the serving bowl.

Nutrition Values: Calories 99, fat 2.9, fiber 1.1, carbs 13.6, protein 4.9

GARLIC PUMPKIN SEEDS

Preparation Time: 5 minutes

Cooking Time: 10 minutes

Servings: 6

Ingredients:

- 1 ½ cup pumpkin seeds
- 3 teaspoons garlic powder
- ½ teaspoon chipotle chili pepper
- 1 teaspoon salt
- 1 tablespoon olive oil

Directions:

1. Place pumpkin seeds in the instant pot.

2. Set Saute mode and cook them for 5 minutes. Stir pumpkin seeds every 1 minute.

3. After this, sprinkle the seeds with olive oil, chipotle chili pepper, salt, and garlic powder.

4. Mix up well and cook for 4 minutes more.

5. Then switch off the instant pot and let seeds rest for 1 minute.

Nutrition Values: Calories 212, fat 18.2, fiber 1.6, carbs 7.3, protein 8.7

FLATBREAD

Preparation Time: 10 minutes

Cooking Time: 5 minutes

Servings: 5

Ingredients:

- 1 cup wheat flour
- 1 teaspoon salt
- ¼ cup of water
- ¾ cup olive oil

Directions:

1. In the mixing bowl mix up together salt, water, and wheat flour.

2. Add olive oil and knead the soft and non-sticky dough.

3. Preheat instant pot on Saute mode well.

4. Meanwhile, cut dough into 5 buns and roll them up to make rounds.

5. Roast dough rounds in the instant pot for 1 minute from each side.

6. Cover cooked flatbreads with the cloth towel till serving.

Nutrition Values: Calories 350, fat 30.5, fiber 0.7, carbs 19.1, protein 2.6

POLENTA FRIES

Preparation Time: 15 minutes

Cooking Time: 10 minutes

Servings: 10

Ingredients:

- 1 cup polenta
- 3 cups almond milk
- 1 teaspoon salt
- 1 teaspoon ground black pepper
- 1 teaspoon dried cilantro
- ½ teaspoon ground cumin
- 1 tablespoon almond butter
- 1 tablespoon olive oil

Directions:

1. Place polenta in the instant pot. Add almond milk and salt.
2. Then add ground black pepper, dried cilantro, and ground cumin. Mix it up.
3. Close and seal the lid.
4. Cook polenta for 6 minutes on High-pressure mode. Allow natural pressure release for 10 minutes.
5. Open the lid and add almond butter. Mix up it well.
6. Transfer the polenta into the square pan and flatten well.
7. Let it chill until solid.
8. Then cut solid polenta onto 10 sticks.
9. Brush every stick with the olive oil.
10. Clean and preheat instant pot on Saute mode until hot.
11. Then cook polenta sticks for 1 minute from each side or until light brown.
12. Chill the snack before serving.

Nutrition Values: Calories 244, fat 19.6, fiber 2.2, carbs 16.7, protein 3.2

GREEN CROQUETTES

Preparation Time: 15 minutes

Cooking Time: 5 minutes

Servings: 4

Ingredients:

- 2 sweet potatoes, peeled, boiled
- 1 cup fresh spinach
- 1 tablespoons peanuts
- 3 tablespoons flax meal
- 1 teaspoon salt
- 1 teaspoon ground black pepper
- 1 tablespoon olive oil
- ½ teaspoon dried oregano
- ¾ cup wheat flour

Directions:

1. Mash the sweet potatoes and place them in the mixing bowl. Add flax meal salt, dried oregano, and ground black pepper.
2. Then blend the spinach with peanuts until smooth.
3. Add the green mixture in the sweet potato.
4. Mix up the mass.
5. Make medium size croquettes and coat them in the wheat flour.
6. Preheat instant pot on Saute mode well.
7. Add olive oil.
8. Roast croquettes for 1 minute from each side or until golden brown.
9. Dry the cooked croquettes with a paper towel if needed.

Nutrition Values: Calories 155, fat 6.8, fiber 2.7, carbs 20.6, protein 4.4

CIGAR BOREK

Preparation Time: 10 minutes

Cooking Time: 5 minutes

Servings: 6

Ingredients:

- 6 oz phyllo dough
- 8 oz vegan Parmesan, grated
- 1 tablespoon vegan mayonnaise
- 1 teaspoon minced garlic
- 1 tablespoon avocado oil

Directions:

1. In the mixing bowl, mix up together grated Parmesan, vegan mayonnaise, and minced garlic.
2. Then cut phyllo dough into triangles.
3. Spread the triangles with cheese mixture and roll in the shape of cigars.
4. Preheat avocado oil in the instant pot on Saute mode.
5. Place rolled "cigar" in the instant pot and cook them for 1-2 minutes or until they are golden brown.

Nutrition Values: Calories 210, fat 2.6, fiber 0.7, carbs 23.1, protein 17.5

FLAKED CLUSTERS

Preparation Time: 10 minutes

Cooking Time: 4 minutes

Servings: 4

Ingredients:

- 3 oz chia seeds
- ½ cup pumpkin seeds
- 1 cup coconut flakes
- 1/3 cup maple syrup
- 1 cup water, for cooking

Directions:

1. In the mixing bowl mix up together chia seeds, pumpkin seeds, coconut flakes, and maple syrup.
2. Then line the trivet with the baking paper.
3. Pour water in the instant pot. Insert lined trivet.
4. With the help of 2 spoons make medium size clusters (patties) from the coconut mixture and put them on the trivet.
5. Close and seal the lid.
6. Cook clusters for 4 minutes on High.
7. Then use quick pressure release and open the lid.
8. Transfer the cooked clusters on the plate and let them chill well.

Nutrition Values: Calories 336, fat 21.2, fiber 9.8, carbs 32.7, protein 8.4

CHICKPEA CRACKERS

Preparation Time: 10 minutes

Cooking Time: 5 minutes

Servings: 4

Ingredients:

- 1 cup chickpeas, cooked
- 1 teaspoon ground coriander
- 1 teaspoon cumin

- 1 teaspoon salt
- ½ teaspoon sesame seeds
- ¼ cup wheat flour
- 1 cup water, for cooking

Directions:

1. Put chickpeas, ground coriander, cumin, and salt in the blender.
2. Blend the mixture until smooth and transfer it in the mixing bowl.
3. Add wheat flour and sesame seeds. Mix it up with the help of a spoon.
4. Then line instant pot baking pan with baking paper.
5. Put chickpea mixture in the pan and flatten it well to get a thin layer.
6. Cut into square pieces.
7. Pour water in the instant pot and insert rack.
8. Place pan with chickpeas mixture on the rack. Close and seal the lid.
9. Cook the crackers for 3 minutes on High-pressure mode. Then use quick pressure release.
10. Open the lid, transfer crackers in the serving bowl and chill well.

Nutrition Values: Calories 215, fat 3.4, fiber 9, carbs 36.6, protein 10.6

EGGPLANT FRIES

Preparation Time: 15 minutes

Cooking Time: 5 minutes

Servings: 4

Ingredients:

- 1 large eggplant
- 1 teaspoon salt

- 2 tablespoons wheat flour
- ½ teaspoon garlic powder
- 1 teaspoon ground black pepper
- 1 cup water, for cooking

Directions:

1. Trim the eggplant and cut it into wedges.
2. Then sprinkle with salt, garlic powder, and ground black pepper. Shake the vegetables well and leave for 5 minutes.
3. After this, coat every eggplant wedge with wheat flour.
4. Pour water in the instant pot, insert trivet.
5. Place pan on the trivet.
6. Transfer eggplant wedges in the pan.
7. Close and seal the instant pot lid.
8. Cook eggplants for 5 minutes on Manual mode (high pressure).
9. Use quick pressure release.
10. Dry the eggplant wedges with the paper towel gently.

Nutrition Values: Calories 45, fat 0.3, fiber 4.3, carbs 10.3, protein 1.6

CRUNCHY ARTICHOKE HEARTS

Preparation Time: 15 minutes

Cooking Time: 10 minutes

Servings: 2

Ingredients:

- 1/3 cup artichoke hearts, canned
- ½ cup panko bread crumbs
- ¼ cup almond milk

- 1 tablespoon flax meal
- 1 teaspoon paprika
- 2 tablespoons sesame oil

Directions:

1. Whisk together almond milk and flax meal.
2. Add paprika and stir well.
3. Then dip artichoke hearts into the almond milk mixture and coat in the panko bread crumbs.
4. Pour sesame oil in the instant pot.
5. Preheat it on saute mode.
6. Place coated artichoke hearts in the instant pot and cook them for 2 minutes from each side.

Nutrition Values: Calories 329, fat 23.7, fiber 5.8, carbs 26.2, protein 6

SCALLION PANCAKES

Preparation Time: 10 minutes

Cooking Time: 5 minutes

Servings: 4

Ingredients:

- ½ cup scallions, chopped
- 2 tablespoons flax meal
- 4 tablespoons water
- 1 teaspoon salt
- 1 potato, peeled, boiled
- 1 tablespoon olive oil
- 1 teaspoon ground black pepper

Directions:

1. Mix up together flax meal and water. Whisk it.

2. Add chopped scallions, salt, and ground black pepper.
3. After this, mash potato and add it in the scallions mixture.
4. Stir it well.
5. Make the balls from the mixture and press them to get pancake shape.
6. Pour olive oil in the instant pot. Preheat it on Saute mode.
7. Add scallions pancakes and cook them for 2 minutes from each side.

Nutrition Values: Calories 83, fat 4.8, fiber 2.4, carbs 9.7, protein 1.9

MUSHROOM ARANCINI

Preparation Time: 10 minutes

Cooking Time: 6 minutes

Servings: 8

Ingredients:

- ½ cup mushrooms, chopped, fried
- ½ cup of rice, cooked
- ½ onion, minced
- ¼ teaspoon minced garlic
- 4 oz vegan Parmesan, grated
- 3 tablespoons flax meal
- 5 tablespoons almond milk
- ¼ cup olive oil
- 1 cup bread crumbs

Directions:

1. Put chopped mushrooms, rice, minced onion, garlic, and grated cheese in the blender.
2. Blend the mixture for 30 seconds.

3. After this, transfer it in the mixing bowl.

4. In the separated bowl whisk together almond milk and flax meal.

5. Add the flax meal mixture in the rice mixture and stir well.

6. Pour olive oil in the instant pot and bring it to boil on Saute mode.

7. Meanwhile, make balls from the rice mixture and coat them in the bread crumbs well.

8. Place the mushroom balls in the hot olive oil and cook for 3 minutes or until light brown.

9. Dry the snack with the paper towel.

Nutrition Values: Calories 230, fat 10.3, fiber 1.9, carbs 23.9, protein 9.4

COATED HEART OF PALM

Preparation Time: 10 minutes

Cooking Time: 25 minutes

Servings: 4

Ingredients:

- 1 cup heart of palm
- ¼ cup wheat flour
- ½ teaspoon salt
- 1 teaspoon maple syrup
- ½ teaspoon paprika
- ½ teaspoon soy sauce
- ¼ cup coconut flakes
- 2 tablespoon sesame oil

Directions:

1. Mix up together wheat flour, salt, paprika, and coconut flakes.

2. In the separated bowl, mix up together the heart of palm, maple syrup, and soy sauce. Stir gently.

3. Toss the heart of palm in the coconut flakes mixture and coat well.

4. Pour sesame oil in the instant pot and preheat it on Saute mode.

5. Cook coated heart of palm in the hot oil for 2 minutes. Then dry with the help of the paper towel.

6. Serve the snack with your favorite vegan sauce.

Nutrition Values: Calories 122, fat 8.8, fiber 1.7, carbs 9.7, protein 2

SWEET TOFU CUBES

Preparation Time: 10 minutes

Cooking Time: 40 minutes

Servings: 2

Ingredients:

- 6 oz firm tofu, cubed
- 1 teaspoon mustard
- 1 teaspoon olive oil
- 1 teaspoon apple cider vinegar
- ½ teaspoon maple syrup

Directions:

1. Place tofu in the instant pot.

2. Sprinkle it with mustard, olive oil, apple cider vinegar, and maple syrup.

3. Mix up the mixture well.

4. Close and seal the lid.

5. Cook tofu cubes for 2 minutes on High-pressure mode.

6. Then use quick pressure release.

7. Transfer the tofu cubes on the serving plate and sprinkle with the remaining gravy.

8. Insert a toothpick in every tofu cube.

Nutrition Values: Calories 92, fat 6.4, fiber 1, carbs 3.2, protein 7.4

DESSERTS

SNICKERDOODLE BARS

Preparation Time: 25 minutes

Cooking Time: 15 minutes

Servings: 4

Ingredients:

- ¼ cup maple syrup
- 1 tablespoon applesauce
- ½ teaspoon vanilla extract
- 2 tablespoons coconut flour
- 1 cup wheat flour
- 1 teaspoon baking powder
- 1 tablespoon candied oranges, chopped
- 2 tablespoons brown sugar
- 1 tablespoon ground cinnamon
- ¼ teaspoon ground cardamom
- ½ cup of water

Directions:

1. In the big mixing bowl, mix up together maple syrup, applesauce, vanilla extract, coconut flour, wheat flour, and baking powder.
2. Mix up the mixture well with the help of the spoon.
3. Then add candied oranges and knead the soft dough.
4. Line the instant pot pan with the baking paper.
5. Pour water and insert trivet in the instant pot.
6. Put the dough in the prepared pan and flatten it.
7. Then sprinkle it with ground cinnamon, cardamom, and brown sugar.
8. Cover the pan with foil and transfer on the trivet. Close and seal the lid.
9. Cook the dessert for 15 minutes on high-pressure mode.
10. Then allow natural pressure release for 10 minutes.
11. Chill the dessert and cut into bars.

Nutrition Values: Calories 219, fat 0.8, fiber 3.4, carbs 49.8, protein 3.8

CINNAMON SWIRLS

Preparation Time: 60 minutes

Cooking Time: 25 minutes

Servings: 6

Ingredients:

- 1 teaspoon nutritional yeast
- 1 cup of soy milk
- ½ cup of water
- ¾ teaspoon salt
- 2 tablespoons white sugar
- 1 ½ cup wheat flour
- ½ cup of rice flour
- 2 tablespoons ground cinnamon
- 2 tablespoons brown sugar
- 2 tablespoons coconut oil
- 1 cup water, for cooking

Directions:

1. Set Saute mode and preheat the soy

milk little bit.

2. Then mix up together white sugar, nutritional yeast, and ½ cup wheat flour.

3. Cover the mixture and leave it in a warm place for 20 minutes.

4. After this, add salt, water, remaining wheat flour, rice flour, and coconut oil.

5. Knead the soft dough. If the dough is sticky: add olive oil.

6. Leave the dough for 20 minutes in warm place.

7. Then pour water in the instant pot. Insert the rack inside.

8. Line the springform pan with baking paper.

9. In the separated bowl, mix up together brown sugar and ground cinnamon.

10. Roll up the dough and sprinkle the surface of it with the ground cinnamon mix.

11. Roll the dough to get the long log.

12. Cut the log into 6 buns and press them gently.

13. Place the buns (swirls) in the prepared springform pan and cover with foil.

14. Secure the edges of the foil and pin small holes on the surface.

15. Transfer the pan on the rack. Close and seal the lid.

16. Cook the cinnamon swirls for 25 minutes on High-pressure mode. Then allow natural pressure release for 10 minutes.

Nutrition Values: Calories 257, fat 5.8, fiber 2.8, carbs 46, protein 5.7

TURMERIC LOAF

Preparation Time: 35 minutes

Cooking Time: 25 minutes

Servings: 8

Ingredients:

- 6 oz coconut flakes
- 1 cup almond milk
- 1 cup wheat flour
- 1 teaspoon vanilla extract
- ¾ cup of sugar
- 1 teaspoon ground cinnamon
- 2 tablespoons turmeric
- 2 bananas, chopped
- 1 teaspoon baking soda
- 1 tablespoon apple cider vinegar
- 1 cup of water

Directions:

1. In the blender: blend together coconut flakes, almond milk, vanilla extract, sugar, and ground cinnamon.

2. Pour the blended liquid in the mixing bowl.

3. Add wheat flour, turmeric, baking soda, and apple cider vinegar.

4. Mix up the loaf batter with the help of the spoon.

5. Pour the batter in the loaf mold.

6. Pour water in the instant pot, insert the trivet.

7. Place loaf mold on the trivet, close and seal the lid.

8. Cook the turmeric loaf for 25 minutes. Then allow natural pressure

release for 20 minutes.

9. Transfer the loaf on the plate and slice.

Nutrition Values: Calories 306, fat 14.7, fiber 4.3, carbs 43.7, protein 3.5

SEMOLINA HALWA

Preparation Time: 10 minutes

Cooking Time: 8 minutes

Servings: 4

Ingredients:

- 2 teaspoons olive oil
- 1 cup semolina
- ½ cup peanuts, chopped
- 4 dates, pitted, chopped
- 4 tablespoons brown sugar
- 1 cup of water
- ½ teaspoon ground cinnamon
- ½ teaspoon ground cardamom
- ¼ teaspoon ground cloves
- ¼ cup dried cranberries, chopped

Directions:

1. Pour olive oil in the instant pot.
2. Add semolina, peanuts, and pitted dates.
3. Start to cook ingredients for 3-4 minutes on Saute mode. Stir them from time to time.
4. After this, add brown sugar, ground cinnamon, cardamom, and ground cloves. Mix up well.
5. Add water and cranberries.
6. With the help of the wooden spatula, mix up semolina mixture very well.
7. Close and seal the instant pot lid.
8. Cook halwa for 4 minutes. Allow natural pressure release for 10 minutes.
9. Open the lid, mix up cooked halwa well and transfer into the small serving ramekins.

Nutrition Values: Calories 337, fat 11.8, fiber 4.4, carbs 49.5, protein 10.3

212. PECAN PIE

Preparation Time: 15 minutes

Cooking Time: 15 minutes

Servings: 4

Ingredients:

- ½ cup wheat flour
- ½ cup coconut butter
- 2 tablespoons brown sugar
- 1 cup pecans, chopped
- ½ cup white sugar
- ¼ cup almond milk
- 1 cup water, for cooking

Directions:

1. Make the sable: mix up together wheat flour, coconut butter, and brown sugar. Knead the soft dough.
2. After this, place the dough in the cake mold and flatten the dough to get the shape of pie crust.
3. Pour water in the instant pot and insert trivet.
4. Place the mold with pie crust on the trivet and close the lid.

5. Set manual mode (high pressure) and cook pie crust for 5 minutes. Allow natural pressure release for 10 minutes.

6. Then open the lid, transfer the mold with pie crust on the chopping board and let it chill.

7. After this, clean the instant pot and discard the trivet.

8. Place inside the instant pot white sugar and almond milk.

9. Melt the mixture on Saute mode.

10. When the sugar mass starts to boil, add chopped pecans and stir well.

11. Switch off the instant pot.

12. Remove the pie crust from the mold.

13. Place the cooked sugar pecans on it and flatten gently.

14. Chill it little.

Nutrition Values: Calories 441, fat 27.2, fiber 6.5, carbs 50.2, protein 4.7

WARM AROMATIC LASSI

Preparation Time: 5 minutes

Cooking Time: 5 minutes

Servings: 2

Ingredients:

- ½ cup almond yogurt
- ½ cup of water
- 2 tablespoons white sugar
- 1 pinch saffron
- ¾ teaspoon ground cardamom
- 1 tablespoon pistachios, chopped

Directions:

1. Preheat instant pot on saute mode.

2. Then add water and boil it.

3. Then add sugar and stir it until dissolved. Pour sweet water in the glass jar.

4. After this, mix up together almond yogurt and water. Whisk the mixture carefully to get homogenous liquid.

5. Sprinkle the liquid with ground cinnamon and saffron. Add ground cardamom. Stir it.

6. Sprinkle the lassi with pistachios and pour into the serving glasses.

Nutrition Values: Calories 100, fat 3.2, fiber 0.9, carbs 17.8, protein 1.5

TOFFEE

Preparation Time: 10 minutes

Cooking Time: 5 minutes

Servings: 2

Ingredients:

- ¼ cup almond butter
- ¼ cup brown sugar
- 1 tablespoon peanuts, chopped
- ½ teaspoon vanilla extract
- 3 oz vegan chocolate chips

Directions:

1. Place sugar and almond butter in the instant pot.

2. Melt the mixture on Saute mode.

3. Line the tray with parchment.

4. Pour the melted mixture on the parchment and spread it.

5. Then sprinkle it with chopped peanuts and chocolate chips.

6. Place the parchment in the freezer for 5-10 minutes.

7. Then remove it from the freezer break into medium size pieces.

Nutrition Values: Calories 337, fat 14.7, fiber 3.4, carbs 47.4, protein 4.5

PEAR COMPOTE

Preparation Time: 10 minutes

Cooking Time: 6 minutes

Servings: 4

Ingredients:

- 4 pears, trimmed
- 1 cup of water
- 1 cinnamon stick
- ¼ teaspoon ground ginger
- 1 tablespoon sugar

Directions:

1. Cut the pears into halves and remove seeds. Chop the fruits.

2. Place them in the instant pot.

3. Add cinnamon stick, ground ginger, water, and sugar.

4. Close and seal the lid.

5. Set Manual mode and cook compote for 6 minutes. Then use quick pressure release.

6. Open the lid and pour the cooked dessert into 4 bowls. Chill well.

Nutrition Values: Calories 265, fat 0.6, fiber 13, carbs 69.8, protein 1.5

CREAM PIE PUDDING

Preparation Time: 15 minutes

Cooking Time: 10 minutes

Servings: 5

Ingredients:

- 2 cups cashew milk
- 1 tablespoon vanilla extract
- 1 tablespoon corn flour
- 1 teaspoon cornstarch
- 4 oz vegan raw chocolate, chopped
- ½ cup of coconut milk
- 1/3 cup sugar
- 2 tablespoons coconut flakes

Directions:

1. Mix up together cashew milk, vanilla extract, corn flour, cornstarch, and sugar.

2. Pour the liquid in the blender and blend it for 15 seconds.

3. Preheat the instant pot on Saute mode until hot.

4. Pour cashew milk mixture in the instant pot. Boil the liquid until it thickens.

5. Then pour the pudding in the bowl.

6. After this, clean the instant pot and place raw chocolate inside.

7. Add coconut milk and saute the mixture until homogenous.

8. Then make the last preparations of the dessert: take the glass jars and pour small inside of the cashew milk pudding inside.

9. Then add melted chocolate mixture.

10. Repeat the steps until you use all the mixtures.

11. Chill the pudding.

Nutrition Values: Calories 267, fat 16.2, fiber 8.1, carbs 28.6, protein 1.5

BANANA CAKE

Preparation Time: 15 minutes

Cooking Time: 7 minutes

Servings: 4

Ingredients:

- 5 bananas, peeled
- 6 oz rice flour
- 1 teaspoon vanilla extract
- 1 tablespoon brown sugar
- 1 tablespoon peanut butter
- Cooking spray
- 1 cup water, for cooking

Directions:

1. Chop the bananas and place them in the mixing bowl.
2. Mash the fruits with the help of the fork.
3. After this, add rice flour, vanilla extract, and brown sugar.
4. Mix up the mixture well.
5. Spray the springform pan with cooking spray and pour banana mixture in it.
6. Pour water in the instant pot, insert trivet; place springform pan on the trivet.
7. Close and seal the lid. Cook the cake for 7 minutes.
8. Then allow natural pressure release for 10 minutes.
9. Spread the cooked cake with peanut butter and cut into slices.

Nutrition Values: Calories 322, fat 3.1, fiber 5.1, carbs 70.9, protein 5.1

CARAMBOLA IN CHAI SYRUP

Preparation Time: 15 minutes

Cooking Time: 6 minutes

Servings: 2

Ingredients:

- 2 cups carambola, sliced
- ½ cup chai syrup
- 1/3 cup water
- ¼ teaspoon ground ginger

Directions:

1. In the instant pot mix up together chai syrup and water.
2. Add ground ginger.
3. Set Saute mode and cook the liquid for 5 minutes.
4. Then add sliced carambola stir gently and cook for 1 minute more.
5. Switch off the instant pot and let carambol soak the syrup.

Nutrition Values: Calories 52, fat 0.4, fiber 3.1, carbs 11.9, protein 1.1

SEMOLINA PUDDING WITH MANGO

Preparation Time: 15 minutes

Cooking Time: 10 minutes

Servings: 4

Ingredients:

- 2 cups almond milk
- ½ cup semolina

- 4 oz mango puree
- 3 tablespoons brown sugar
- 1 teaspoon vanilla extract
- 1 teaspoon coconut oi

Directions:

1. l
2. Pour almond milk in the instant pot and preheat it on Saute mode.
3. When it starts to boil, add semolina, brown sugar, and vanilla extract.
4. Bring it to boil again. Stir well.
5. Then close the lid and switch off the instant pot.
6. Leave it for 10 minutes.
7. After this, add coconut oil and stir well.
8. Place mango puree in the serving bowls.
9. Add semolina pudding over the puree.

Nutrition Values: Calories 404, fat 30, fiber 3.7, carbs 32.1, protein 5.5

WALNUT SWEETS

Preparation Time: 5 minutes

Cooking Time: 5 minutes

Servings: 4

Ingredients:

- 1 cup walnuts kernels
- 4 oz vegan raw chocolate, chopped
- ¾ cup almond milk

Directions:

1. Preheat instant pot on Saute mode until hot.
2. Add chopped raw chocolate and cook it for 2 minutes.
3. When it is melted, add almond milk and whisk until homogenous.
4. Then coat the walnut kernels in the chocolate mixture.
5. Line the tray with the baking paper.
6. Transfer the coated chocolate walnuts on the prepared tray. Let the sweets dry.
7. Stor the walnut sweets in the closed paper box.

Nutrition Values: Calories 459, fat 40.3, fiber 12.2, carbs 19.8, protein 9.6

BLUEBERRY BROWNIES.

Preparation Time: 20 Minutes

Servings: 8

Ingredients:

- 1 cup cooked black beans
- ¾ cup unbleached all-purpose flour
- ½ cup unsweetened cocoa powder
- ½ cup blueberry jam
- ½ cup natural sugar
- 1½ teaspoons baking powder
- 1 teaspoon pure vanilla extract

Directions:

1. Lightly oil a baking tray that will fit in the steamer basket of your Instant Pot.
2. Blend together the beans, cocoa, jam, sugar, and vanilla.
3. Fold in the flour and baking powder

until the batter is smooth.

4. Pour the batter into your tray and put the tray in your steamer basket.

5. Pour the minimum amount of water into the base of your Instant Pot and lower the steamer basket.

6. Seal and cook on Steam for 12 minutes.

7. Release the pressure quickly and set to one side to cool a little before slicing.

PUMPKIN SPICE OAT BARS.

Preparation Time: 25 Minutes

Servings: 10

Ingredients:

- 2 cups old-fashioned rolled oats
- 1 cup non-dairy milk
- 2/3 cup canned solid-pack pumpkin
- ½ cup chopped toasted pecans
- ½ cup sweetened dried cranberries
- ½ cup packed light brown sugar or granulated natural sugar
- 6 ounces soft or silken tofu, drained and crumbled
- 2 teaspoons ground cinnamon
- 1½ teaspoons baking powder
- 1 teaspoon salt
- 1 teaspoon pure vanilla extract
- ¼ teaspoon ground nutmeg
- ¼ teaspoon ground allspice

Directions:

1. Lightly oil a baking tray that will fit in the steamer basket of your Instant Pot.

2. Stir together the oats, cinnamon, nutmeg, allspice, sugar, baking powder, and salt.

3. Blend together the tofu, pumpkin, milk, and vanilla until smooth and even.

4. Stir the wet and dry ingredients together before folding in the pecans and cranberries.

5. Pour the batter into your tray and put the tray in your steamer basket.

6. Pour the minimum amount of water into the base of your Instant Pot and lower the steamer basket.

7. Seal and cook on Steam for 12 minutes.

8. Release the pressure quickly and set to one side to cool a little before slicing.

TUTTIFRUTTI COBBLER.

Preparation Time: 30 Minutes

Servings: 6

Ingredients:

- 1¼ cups unbleached all-purpose flour
- 1 cup fresh blueberries, rinsed and picked over
- 1 cup fresh blackberries, rinsed and picked over
- ¾ cup natural sugar
- ½ cup unsweetened almond milk
- 2 large ripe peaches, peeled, pitted, and sliced
- 2 ripe apricots, peeled, pitted, and sliced

- 1½ tablespoons tapioca starch or cornstarch
- 1 tablespoon vegetable oil
- 1 teaspoon baking powder
- ½ teaspoon pure vanilla extract
- ¼ teaspoon salt
- ¼ teaspoon ground cinnamon

Directions:

1. Lightly oil a baking tray that will fit in the steamer basket of your Instant Pot.
2. Toss the fruit in the tapioca and ½ a cup of sugar and put in the tray.
3. Put the tray in your steamer basket.
4. Pour the minimum amount of water into the base of your Instant Pot and lower the steamer basket.
5. Seal and cook on Steam for 12 minutes.
6. In a bowl stir together the flour, remaining sugar, cinnamon, baking powder, and salt.
7. Slowly combine with the almond milk, vanilla, and oil until soft dough is formed.
8. Release the Instant Pot's pressure quickly, give the fruit a stir, and cover with the dough.
9. Seal and Steam for another 5 minutes.
10. Release the pressure quickly and set to one side to cool a little.

PEAR MINCEMEAT.

Preparation Time: 35 Minutes

Servings: 6

Ingredients:

- 4 firm ripe Bosc pears, peeled, cored, and chopped
- 1 large orange
- 1½ cups apple juice
- 1¼ cups granola of your choice
- 1 cup raisins (dark, golden, or a combination)
- 1 cup chopped dried apples, pears, or apricots, or a combination
- ½ cup packed dark brown sugar or granulated natural sugar
- ¼ cup brandy or 1 teaspoon brandy extract
- 2 tablespoons pure maple syrup or agave nectar
- 2 tablespoons cider vinegar
- ½ teaspoon ground cinnamon
- ½ teaspoon ground allspice
- ½ teaspoon ground nutmeg
- ¼ teaspoon ground cloves
- Pinch of salt

Directions:

1. Zest the orange, then peel it, deseed it, and quarter it.
2. Blend the orange flesh and zest and put in your Instant Pot.
3. Add the pears, dried fruits, juice, sugar, brandy spices, vinegar, and salt.
4. Seal and cook on Stew for 12 minutes.
5. Release the pressure naturally, take out some of the juice, then reseal and cook another 12 minutes.
6. In a bowl mix the granola and syrup.

7. Release the pressure of the Instant Pot naturally and sprinkle the crumble on top.

8. Seal the Instant Pot and cook on Stew for another 5 minutes.

9. Release the pressure naturally and serve.

BROWN BETTY BANANAS FOSTER.

Preparation Time: 15 Minutes

Servings: 4

Ingredients:

- 6 cups cubed white bread, a little stale helps

- 4 ripe bananas, peeled and chopped

- ⅓cup chopped toasted pecans

- ⅓cup pure maple syrup

- ⅓cup packed light brown sugar or granulated natural sugar

- ¼ cup unsweetened almond milk

- 2 tablespoons brandy

- ½ teaspoon ground cinnamon

- ¼ teaspoon ground nutmeg

- ¼ teaspoon ground ginger

- ⅛ teaspoon salt

Directions:

Lightly oil a baking tray that will fit in the steamer basket of your Instant Pot.

1. In a bowl combine almond milk, maple syrup, and the spices.

2. Roll the bread cubes in the milk mix.

3. In another bowl mix the bananas, pecans, brandy, and sugar.

4. Layer your two mixes in the tray: half bread, half banana, half bread, half banana.

5. Pour the minimum amount of water into the base of your Instant Pot and lower the steamer basket.

6. Seal and cook on Steam for 12 minutes.

7. Release the pressure quickly and set to one side to cool a little.

BREAD & BUTTER PUDDING.

Preparation Time: 25 Minutes

Servings: 8

Ingredients:

- 3 cups nondairy milk, warmed

- 2 cups cubed spiced bread or cake, stale is better

- 2 cups cubed whole-grain bread, stale is better

- 1 (16-ounce) can solid-pack pumpkin

- ¾ cup packed light brown sugar or granulated natural sugar

- 3 tablespoons rum or bourbon or 1 teaspoon rum extract (optional)

- 1 teaspoon pure vanilla extract

- 1½ teaspoons ground cinnamon

- ¼ teaspoon ground nutmeg

- ¼ teaspoon ground allspice

- ¼ teaspoon ground ginger

- ¼ teaspoon salt

Directions:

1. Lightly oil a baking tray that will fit in the steamer basket of your Instant Pot.

2. Put the bread cubes in the tray.

3. Mix the pumpkin, sugar, vanilla, rum, spices, and salt.

4. Slowly stir in the milk.

5. Pour the mix over the bread.

6. Pour the minimum amount of water into the base of your Instant Pot and lower the steamer basket.

7. Seal and cook on Steam for 20 minutes.

8. Release the pressure quickly and set to one side to cool a little.

CUSTARD BREAD PUDDING.

Preparation Time: 45 Minutes

Servings: 6

Ingredients:

- 6 cups cubed white bread

- 3 cups unsweetened almond milk

- 2 cups fresh raspberries or sliced strawberries, for serving

- ½ cup vegan white chocolate chips

- ½ cup packed light brown sugar or granulated natural sugar

- ½ cup dry Marsala

- Pinch of salt

Directions:

1. Melt your white chocolate into a cup of the almond milk. If using your Instant Pot, keep the lid off, stir throughout.

2. Add the Marsala, sugar, and salt.

3. Clean your Instant Pot.

4. Press half the bread cubes into the insert.

5. Pour half the Marsala mix on top.

6. Repeat.

7. Seal and cook on low for 35 minutes.

8. Release the pressure naturally.

9. Serve warm with fresh berries.

CHOCOLATE BREAD PUDDING.

Preparation Time: 40 Minutes

Servings: 6

Ingredients:

- 4 cups white bread cubes

- 2 cups unsweetened almond milk

- 2 cups vegan semisweet chocolate chips

- ½ cup chopped pecans or walnuts

- ¾ cup granulated natural sugar

- ¼ cup unsweetened cocoa powder

- 1 tablespoon vegan butter

- 1 teaspoon pure vanilla extract

- ½ teaspoon salt

Directions:

1. Oil a baking tray that will fit in your Instant Pot.

2. Melt 1 and 2/3 of the chocolate chips with 1.5 cups of the almond milk.

3. Spread the bread cubes in your Instant Pot, sprinkle with nuts, and the remaining chocolate chips.

4. Warm the remaining almond milk in another saucepan with the sugar, cocoa, vanilla, and salt.

5. Combine the cocoa mix with the chocolate chip mix and pour it over the bread.

6. Seal your Instant Pot and cook on Beans for 30 minutes.

7. Depressurize naturally.

MANGO RICE PUDDING.

Preparation Time: 35 Minutes

Servings: 6

Ingredients:

- 2 (14-ounce) cans unsweetened coconut milk

- 2 cups unsweetened almond milk, plus more if needed

- 1 cup uncooked jasmine rice

- ½ cup granulated natural sugar, or more to taste

- 1 large ripe mango, peeled, pitted, and chopped

- 1 teaspoon coconut extract

- 1 teaspoon pure vanilla extract

- ¼ teaspoon salt

Directions:

1. Spray the Instant Pot insert with cooking spray.

2. Add the milks and bring to a boil.

3. Add the rice, sugar, and salt, seal, and cook on Rice.

4. Depressurize quickly and stir in the extracts and mango.

5. The pudding will thicken as it cools.

TAPIOCA WITH APRICOTS.

Preparation Time: 25 Minutes

Servings: 4

Ingredients:

- 2½ cups unsweetened almond milk

- ½ cup chopped dried apricots

- ⅓ cup small pearl tapioca

- ⅓ cup granulated natural sugar

- ¼ cup apricot preserves

- 1 teaspoon pure vanilla extract

Directions:

1. Spray the inside of your Instant Pot with cooking spray.

2. Put in the tapioca, sugar, almond milk, and apricots.

3. Seal and cook on Stew for 12 minutes.

4. Release the pressure fast.

5. In a bowl combine the preserve and vanilla.

6. Add the mixture to your tapioca and reseal your Instant Pot.

7. Leave to finish in its own heat.

8. Serve hot or cold.

POACHED PEARS IN GINGER SAUCE.

Preparation Time: 25 Minutes

Servings: 6

Ingredients:

- 2½ cups white grape juice

- 6 firm ripe cooking pears, peeled, halved, and cored

- ¼ cup natural sugar, plus more if needed

- 6 strips lemon zest

- ½ cinnamon stick

- 2 teaspoons grated fresh ginger
- Juice of 1 lemon
- Pinch of salt

Directions:

1. Warm the grape juice, ginger, lemon zest, salt, and sugar until blended.
2. Add the cinnamon stick and the pears.
3. Seal and cook on Stew for 12 minutes.
4. Take the pears out.
5. Add lemon juice and more sugar to the liquid.
6. Cook with the lid off a few minutes to thicken.
7. Serve.

BAKED" APPLES.

Preparation Time: 35 Minutes

Servings: 6

Ingredients:

- 6 large firm Granny Smith apples, washed
- ½ cup naturally sweetened cranberry juice
- ⅓ cup sweetened dried cranberries
- ⅓ cup packed light brown sugar or granulated natural sugar
- ¼ cup crushed, chopped, or coarsely ground almonds, walnuts, or pecans
- Juice of 1 lemon
- ½ teaspoon ground cinnamon

Directions:

1. Core the apples most of the way

down, leaving a little base so the stuffing stays put.

2. Stand your apples upright in your Instant Pot. Do not pile them on top of each other! You may need to do two batches.
3. In a bowl combine the sugar, nuts, cranberries, and cinnamon.
4. Stuff each apple with the mix.
5. Pour the cranberry juice around the apples.
6. Seal and cook on Stew for 20 minutes.
7. Depressurize naturally.

MAPLE & RUM APPLES.

Preparation Time: 25 Minutes

Servings: 6

Ingredients:

- 6 Granny Smith apples, washed
- ½ cup pure maple syrup
- ½ cup apple juice
- ⅓ cup packed light brown sugar
- ¼ cup golden raisins
- ¼ cup dark rum or spiced rum
- ¼ cup old-fashioned rolled oats
- ¼ cup macadamia nut pieces
- 1 teaspoon ground cinnamon
- ½ teaspoon ground nutmeg
- Juice of 1 lemon

Directions:

1. Core the apples most of the way down, leaving a little base so the stuffing stays put.

2. Stand your apples upright in your Instant Pot. Do not pile them on top of each other! You may need to do two batches.

3. In a bowl combine the oats, sugar, raisins, nuts, and half the nutmeg, half the cinnamon.

4. Stuff each apple with the mix.

5. In another bowl combine the remaining nutmeg and cinnamon, the maple syrup, and the rum.

6. Pour the glaze over the apples.

7. Seal and cook on Stew for 20 minutes.

8. Depressurize naturally.

PUMPKIN & CHOCOLATE LOAF.

Preparation Time: 15 Minutes

Servings: 8

Ingredients:

- 1¾ cups unbleached all-purpose flour
- 1 cup canned solid-pack pumpkin
- ½ cup packed light brown sugar or granulated natural sugar
- ½ cup semisweet vegan chocolate chips
- ¼ cup pure maple syrup
- 2 tablespoons vegetable oil
- 2 teaspoons baking powder
- 1 teaspoon pure vanilla extract
- ½ teaspoon salt
- ½ teaspoon ground cinnamon
- ¼ teaspoon ground allspice
- ¼ teaspoon ground nutmeg

Directions:

1. Lightly oil a baking tray that will fit in the steamer basket of your Instant Pot.

2. In a bowl, combine the flour, baking powder, baking soda, salt and spices.

3. In another bowl combine the pumpkin, maple syrup, sugar, vanilla, and oil.

4. Stir the wet mixture into the dry mixture slowly until they form a smooth mix.

5. Fold in the chocolate chips.

6. Pour the batter into your baking tray and put the tray in your steamer basket.

7. Pour the minimum amount of water into the base of your Instant Pot and lower the steamer basket.

8. Seal and cook on Steam for 10 minutes.

9. Release the pressure quickly and set to one side to cool a little.

CONCLUSION

Certainly, you are now feeling motivated and ready to eat healthy Vegan foods which will help you achieve your ideal body and make a positive impact on the earth and all its' inhabitance. A lifestyle changes that, I hope will be a good fit for you and that you will stick to from now henceforth.

However, it is important to note that lifestyle changes are a process that takes a lot of time getting used to and you, therefore, require support. The fact that you are now ready to make a change is a huge step; the difficult part usually comes in committing and following through with your goals.

Here are a few tips that can set you on the right path of success.

Make a plan that you can follow through

Look at your plan as a road map that is supposed to guide you on this amazing journey of change. Don't stress too much about it. Look at it like an adventure that is going to impact positively on your life. Be specific with every plan you make, and most of all, be realistic. If you plan to lose weight; how much weight do you want to lose and within what period?

Small but sure

The best way to meet your goals is to start small by setting daily goals then let this transform into weekly goals.

Drop one bad habit at a time, don't go cold turkey!

We acquire bad habits over time, and so does replacing them with healthy habits; this is the surest way to success. Take it one habit after another until finally, you start leading a pure Vegan way of life.

All the best!!!